THE THREE
TRAGIC HEROES OF THE
VILNIUS GHETTO
WITENBERG, SHEINBAUM, GENS

To LILY MARGULES,
IN MEMORY OF THE EVENTS THAT
WE WILL NEVER FORGET

X, 2002   N. Shneidy —

ALSO BY N. N. SHNEIDMAN

Literature and Ideology in Soviet Education
Lexington: D.C. Heath and Company, 1973

The Soviet Road to Olympus: Theory and Practice of Soviet Physical Culture
Toronto: OISE Press, 1978

Soviet Literature in the 1970's: Artistic Diversity and Ideological Conformity
Toronto: University of Toronto Press, 1979

Dostoevsky and Suicide, Oakville: Mosaic Press, 1984

Soviet Literature in the 1980's: Decade of Transition
Toronto: University of Toronto Press, 1989

Russian Literature 1988-1994: The End of an Era
Toronto: University of Toronto Press, 1995

Jerusalem of Lithuania: The Rise and Fall of Jewish Vilnius
Oakville: Mosaic Press, 1998

THE THREE

TRAGIC HEROES OF THE
VILNIUS GHETTO

WITENBERG, SHEINBAUM, GENS

N. N. SHNEIDMAN

mosaic press

National Library of Canada Cataloguing in Publication Data

Shneidman, N. N.
    The three tragic heroes of the Vilnius Ghetto: Witenberg,
Sheinbaum, Gens

Includes bibliographical references and index.
ISBN 0-88962-785-1

    1. Holocaust, Jewish (1939-1945) — Lithuania — Vilnius.
2. Witenberg, Yitzhak, 1907-1943. 3. Sheinbaum, Yechiel
4. Gens, Jacob, 1905-1943. I. Title

DS135.L52V543 2002   940.53'18'094793   C2002-900490-X

Published by Mosaic Press, offices and warehouse at 1252 Speers Road, Units 1 and 2, Oakville, Ontario, L6L 5N9, Canada and Mosaic Press, PMB 145, 4500 Witmer Industrial Estates, Niagara Falls, NY, 14305-1386, U.S.A.

Mosaic Press acknowledges the assistance of the Canada Council and the Department of Canadian Heritage, Government of Canada for their support of our publishing programme.

Le Conseil des Arts | The Canada Council
du Canada | for the Arts

Mosaic Press in Canada:
1252 Speers Road, Units 1 & 2,
Oakville, Ontario
L6L 5N9
Phone/Fax: 905-825-2130
mosaicpress@on.aibn.com

Mosaic Press in U.S.A.:
4500 Witmer Industrial Estates
PMB 145, Niagara Falls, NY
14305-1386
Phone/Fax: 1-800-387-8992
mosaicpress@on.aibn.com

Contents

Introduction

THE NAZI GENOCIDE OF THE JEWISH PEOPLE
has become today an important subject of historical investigation and
scrutiny. An impressive body of factual evidence has been amassed to
corroborate the Nazi atrocities all over occupied Europe, and the destruction of the Jewish communities in Poland, Lithuania, Belorussia, and
other occupied regions.

Most recent books about the Holocaust can be divided into several
distinct categories. Some explore the roots of German anti-Semitism,
the reasons which made possible the rise of the Nazis to power, and the
means and methods of the implementation of the so-called "Final Solution." Other historical studies investigate Jewish life in Nazi occupied
Europe, with particular emphasis on the daily existence in ghettos and
concentration camps. The most impressive number of books about the
Holocaust, however, is produced not by scholars or historians, but rather
by Holocaust survivors who provide the reader with accounts of their
personal shocking experiences and memoirs of life under Nazi occupation.

There are also a number of studies which investigate the Jewish
underground resistance to Nazi oppression, and the intricate interrela-
tionship between the Jewish ghetto leaders, and the leaders of the Jewish
underground resistance movements. These individuals influenced, in
different ways, the fate of many Jews under Nazi occupation, and affected
their chances for survival. Many such studies, written mostly by participants of the event discussed, illustrate that both, Jewish ghetto

administrators and underground resistance leaders in the ghetto, wanted to save as many Jews as possible from imminent destruction. They could not agree, however, on a single approach of how best to oppose the Nazi oppression, and devise a common strategy which would help survive as many Jews as possible.

Today, many years after the Holocaust, the story about the Jewish underground resistance movement, and the alleged uprising in the Vilnius ghetto, is still incomplete. Many accounts, provided by former members of the Jewish underground or Jewish ghetto officials in Vilnius, are often limited in scope and relate events from a personal perspective. The views expressed in many post-war studies rather than render an all-round picture of the harrowing past, often reflect the current political and social aims of their authors. Thus, for example, studies of the resistance movement in the Vilnius ghetto, written by citizens of the former Soviet Union, and published in the USSR after the war, place particular emphasis on the contribution of the Communist Party to the resistance movement under Nazi occupation. They hardly mention that most participants of the underground movement in the Vilnius ghetto belonged to other political parties, and that among the underground leaders were many Zionists.

Other authors, mainly those who have settled after the Second World War in Israel, go to other extremes. They often minimize the significance of Soviet involvement in the underground war and fail to stress that without Soviet participation, and the proximity of the front line, any military resistance to Nazi occupation would be meaningless and doomed to failure.

There is also another kind of prejudice, one which reflects the continuous internal political squabbling between different political parties, and social and religious groups in the ghetto, as well as in the post-Second World War Jewish communities. Thus, the seminal account of life in the Vilnius ghetto, *Togbukh fun Vilner geto* (Diary of the Vilna Ghetto /New York 1961/), written during the war by the ghetto librarian and historian, Herman Kruk, could be regarded as one of the most important documents of Jewish life in Vilnius, in the years between 1941 and 1943. Kruk, however, a prominent member of the Yiddishist socialist party *Bund,* could not detach himself from his political and ideological fixation. His picture of the political situation in the ghetto is often one-sided and not always correct. Moreover, he used his pen and position in the ghetto, to attack and denigrate in his diary his political adversaries.

Another important original study, published soon after the war, by Mark Dworzecki , *Yerushalayim de-Lita in kamf un umkum* (Jerusalem of Lithuania in Struggle and Destruction /Paris 1948/) provides a detailed account of Jewish life in Vilnius during the war, with particular attention to the political and resistance movements in the ghetto. The main emphasis in the book, however, is on the clandestine activity of Zionist groups, and the involvement of other political parties in the underground resistance movement is mentioned only in passing.

Similarly, the otherwise informative book by Chaim Lazar, *Resistance and Destruction* (New York 1985), may serve as an example of another kind of political prejudice. It may appear from the book that the main purpose of the author, himself a member of the Zionist-Revisionist party, is to identify and extol the heroism and dedication of every single member of the resistance and partisan movements who was a member of the Zionist-Revisionist organization *Betar*. The achievements of all other participants in the anti-Nazi struggle are to the author of secondary importance.

Today, close to sixty years after the events described, the number of those who are still alive, and can bear witness to the events discussed, diminishes daily. Moreover, most archival material about the Holocaust in Lithuania, previously hidden in secret Soviet repositories, has been uncovered. Thus, it has become possible, and necessary, to reexamine in a detached and objective manner, and without any preconceived political or ideological notions, all available material about the relationship between the leaders of different Jewish underground resistance organizations and their interaction with the leaders of the Jewish ghetto administration.

The objective of this study is to juxtapose the different approaches to the issue of resistance and survival by the three leading figures in the Vilnius ghetto, and to illustrate that the lack of unity in, and coordination of, any anti-Nazi activity in the Jewish community of Vilnius in general, and the internal political and ideological disagreements and rivalry between different underground resistance leaders in the ghetto in particular, hampered not only Jewish anti-Nazi resistance endeavours of the ghetto underground, but in certain instances endangered even the existence of the whole ghetto, and the safety and survival of the Jews still remaining in the city.

The situation in the Vilnius ghetto, and the relationship between armed resistance and survival in the ghetto was, at any time, tenuous at best, because no one, in one's most vivid imagination, could fathom the degree of heinousness and perfidy of the Nazi murderers. Hence, only well planned , organized, and coordinated anti-Nazi activity could bear positive results.

I hope that this study will shed some new light on the relationship between resistance and survival under Nazi occupation, and the connection between ideological indoctrination and practical conduct under Nazi occupation. Moreover, it will stimulate a better understanding of the intricate processes that determine human behaviour and action in conditions of subjugation, tyranny, and extreme cruelty.

The three tragic heroes, discussed in the book, Yitzhak Witenberg, the commander of the F.P.O. (United Partisan Organization), Yechiel Sheinbaum, the leader of the Second Fighting Organization, and Jacob Gens, the Head of the Ghetto, were leading figures in the ghetto underground resistance movement and Jewish ghetto administration accordingly, and the term "tragic hero" is used here as a literary metaphor to designate the life experiences and tragic fates of these three important personalities.

All three, Witenberg, Sheinbaum, and Gens, struggled for survival, but each of them viewed life and Jewish history from a different perspective and favoured a different approach to the resistance to Nazi oppression. The behaviour and actions of the three provoked and incited, at different times, different reactions from the ghetto prisoners, the ghetto administration, as well as the German occupiers. The discussion of their fates illustrates that despite exhaustion, malnutrition, and the constantly lurking death, most residents of the Vilnius ghetto were always alert, ready to resist , and fight for their lives. It demonstrates also that political and ideological differences in the Jewish community were as distinct in ghetto conditions as in times of peace. It hints also at the fact that while, under any circumstances, plurality of opinion is an indispensable tool of democratic government, only compromise and unity of action can lead to political and military success. In many instances the internal adversary can be more dangerous and destructive than the wicked external enemy.

Chapter One of the proposed book provides the historical background for the discussion of the fates of the three tragic heroes. It gives a brief outline of the historical past of the Jewish community of Vilnius, and provides a detailed account of the life in the ghetto from 6 September 1941 to 23 September 1943. Chapters Two-Four are devoted to the discussion and analysis of the personalities of Witenberg, Sheinbaum, and Gens respectively, whose actions were crucial to the fate of the Vilnius ghetto, and affected in different ways the lives and chances for survival of each individual ghetto inhabitant. In the Conclusion the discussion is summarized and the events, as well as the fates of the three tragic heroes, are placed in a broader perspective.

Names of places are usually given in the book in the version commonly used in the English language and appropriate for the historical period under consideration. The designations Vilna, Wilna, Vilno (Wilno), and Vilnius are used interchangeably to reflect the historical realities of the times discussed. One has to bear in mind that with the frequent change of rulers the name of the city would change as well. To avoid confusion it is worth noting that under Russian control the city was called Vilna; under Polish administration — Wilno, and under Lithuanian rule — Vilnius. In German it is Wilna, in Yiddish Vilne, and in Hebrew Vilna. All translations from other languages, unless quoted from English language sources, are my own. I have adopted in the book, with minor exceptions, the widely used transliteration system of the Library of Congress.

A note of thanks is due to my friends and colleagues who read the manuscript and offered constructive criticism. I would like also to express my appreciation to the associates of the Jewish Museum in Vilnius who provided me with the opportunity of becoming acquainted with original archival materials unavailable elsewhere. I acknowledge with gratitude the advice and assistance of all those who helped me in my work, but I accept sole responsibility for any inaccuracies, biases, or mistakes which may exist in the book.

N.N.S.
Toronto, Canada
2002

CHAPTER ONE:
The Ghetto in Vilnius

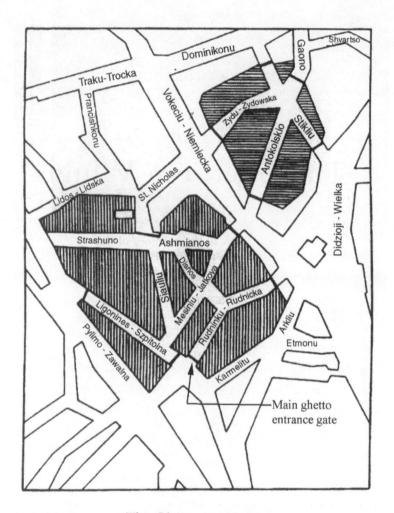

Main ghetto
entrance gate

The Ghetto in Vilnius

 First Ghetto: September 6, 1941 - September 23, 1943

Second Ghetto: September 6, 1941 - October 21, 1941

The Ghetto in Vilnius

THE PROCESS OF THE SEPARATION OF JEWS from their gentile neighbours, in most European countries, is as old as the exile of the Jews from their ancestral home in Israel. Historically ghettos were created to isolate and humiliate the Jewish people, and to indicate their indeterminate status as non-Europeans. Ironically, in some cases, "ghettos of the early medieval era were actually requested by the Jews themselves as a tangible physical symbol of their corporate autonomy."[1] Moreover, ghettos prevented intercourse with gentiles, but afforded its residents a measure of protection from assaults, plunder and violence and were, therefore, not totally unwelcome by them.

Pope Paul IV (1555-1559) created the first "official" ghetto in Rome in 1555. Other Catholic sovereigns in Europe followed Paul's example. The ghetto was usually on the dingiest street, or the most dilapidated part of the medieval town, and except for the expressed purpose of business Jews were forbidden to leave the ghetto. The special quarters to which Jews were consigned were closed off, and the gates, wherever they existed, were locked from night to dawn, as well as on Sundays and Christian holidays. The Jews were thus shut off from the outside world altogether, and the ghetto became a separate world in the physical as well as spiritual sense.

The French Revolution abolished the walls of the ghettos in France and emancipated the Jews from discrimination and degradation. In 1797, after the arrival of the French army in Italy, Jews were granted there complete civil equality as well.[2] Early in the nineteenth century, under the pressure of the French occupying army, the ghetto walls in German cities were burned and demolished and Jewish equality was constitutionalized.

In Eastern Europe, including Poland and Lithuania, Jews were on numerous occasions also forcibly separated from their gentile neighbours. In many towns their movement was restricted, their economic activity limited, and their place of residence confined to designated areas. Originally Russia never had an indigenous Jewish population, and Jews were usually driven out from areas conquered by the Russian army. In 1791 the Russian tsar Catherine II (1762-1796) established the Jewish pale of settlement, in an area delineated by the boundaries of the former Polish Kingdom. By 1794 all Jews in the Russian empire were, in a sense, "ghettoised," confined to the pale of settlement, and forbidden to own land. By 1795 the Polish-Lithuanian Kingdom ceased to exist. It was partitioned between Russia, Germany, and Austro-Hungary and, after 1795, most Jewish inhabitants of Lithuania and Eastern Poland shared in many respects the fate of Russian Jews. The October Revolution of 1917 abolished all tsarist laws and Jews in Russia were free, with certain limitations, to move and settle wherever they wished.

The emancipation of the West European Jews after the French Revolution, and the abolition after the Bolshevik Revolution of the restrictions on Jewish movement and settlement in tsarist Russia, did not imply the complete end of Jewish suffering and subjugation in twentieth century Europe. In November 1935, after the advent of Hitler to power in Germany, the so-called Nuremberg laws were enacted, and basic anti-Jewish racial policy became the order of the day. These laws also provided for the restoration of ghettos. Jews were again subjected to forced labour and deprived of their property and professions. The legal restoration of the ghetto in Germany was not a religious or social undertaking, it was rather the expression of Nazi racist policies which aimed at the gradual and systematic eradication of Jewish life in Germany proper, and the physical and spiritual destruction of German Jewry.

In August 1938 an office for Jewish emigration and resettlement was established in Germany, and the "Final Solution" was set in motion.

On 24 January 1939, Hermann Goering issued an order to Reinhard Heydrich, who was then in charge of the Jewish Emigration Office, concerning the solution of the Jewish question by "emigration" and "evacuation." After the invasion of Poland, in September 1939, Heydrich instructed, the so-called *Einsatzgruppen* (mobile SS units assigned to carry out 'special task'), to combat the civil enemy and persecute the Polish Jews by various means, including mass murder.

It did not take long before the Nazis began to abuse and tyrannize their Jewish subjects. The first ghetto in occupied Poland was established on 28 November 1939 in the city of Piotrkow. It was followed by the creation of ghettos in other Polish cities, including Lodz in the spring of 1940, and Warsaw in October 1940. Early in 1940, on 27 April, Heinrich Himmler issued a directive concerning the establishment of a concentration camp in Auschwitz, and a month later the camp was put in operation. At that time, however, the systematic murder of Jews was not official German policy yet. Indeed, Jews were expelled, deported, victimized in many different ways, and confined to ghettos, but not murdered en masse yet. With time, however, the expression of German Nazi anti-Semitism became more virulent, and prior to the invasion of the Soviet Union, in June 1941, Hitler entrusted Reinhard Heydrich, Chief of the Gestapo and Reich Main Security Office, with the preparation of the so-called "Final Solution" of the Jewish problem. It literally meant the physical destruction of all Jewish people under Nazi jurisdiction by all available means. At that time, however, the secrecy of the operation was still scrupulously guarded.

In March-April 1941, prior to the German assault on the USSR, an agreement was reached between the high command of the German army and the *Reichsfuhrer SS* in which the mission of the *Einsatzgruppen* in the areas of anticipated German-Soviet hostilities was outlined. Their main function was to follow the *Wehrmacht* and murder as many Jews as possible, as soon as possible.

There were four *Einsatzgruppen* with between 500-800 individuals in each. They were composed of people taken from the SS, SD, the Gestapo, and the German military police. Each group was sent to a different region of occupied Eastern Europe. Group "A" operated in the Baltic states, group "B" in Belorussia and Poland, and groups "C" and "D" in the regions of Moldavia, the Ukraine, and the Caucasus.[3]

Einsatzgruppe "A", in the Baltic states, which included the region of Vilnius, was first commanded by the SS Brigade Commander Franz W. Stahlecker. He was replaced, on 24 March 1942, by SS Brigade Commander and Police Major-General Heinz Jost.

Concentration camps, with adjacent crematoria, were to be the main instrument of the "Final Solution." These were the places where extreme exploitation was to be followed by physical extermination in gas chambers. The number of Jews in the territories occupied by Germany in Eastern Europe was, however, so great that it was impossible to kill them all at once. Neither the *Einsatzgruppen*, nor the newly constructed death camp in occupied Poland, could fulfil this task. Hence, the immediate objective of the administration entrusted with the task of implementing the "Final Solution" was to clear the country-side, in occupied Eastern Europe, from its Jewish inhabitants, and incarcerate all remaining Jews in the cities in the newly created ghettos.

It was clear from the outset that the ghettos, created by the Nazis in Eastern Europe, were not intended as an end in itself. They were rather an intermediate stage in the process of the "Final Solution," and only a temporary reprieve for their inhabitants from inevitable destruction. Ghettos were created by the Nazis not only with the purpose of isolating, dehumanizing, degrading, and oppressing their inhabitants, but also to exploit them as a source of cheap labour. There were among the Jews many able-bodied workers, as well as highly qualified tradesmen, professionals, and technicians whose contribution to the German economy and its war effort were very important. The more so since their labour was almost free of charge. The ghetto dwellers were exploited and subjected to exhaustive physical labour and malnutrition. They could live, however, in relative safety only for as long as they were productive, and until their life juices and energies were totally depleted. Then they would become disposable and share the fate of their brethren who were already put to death earlier.

Until the arrival of the Nazis in Vilnius there was a flourishing Jewish community in the city. The Jews of Vilnius had a long history, and the first Jews settled there early in the fourteenth century. Jewish life in Vilnius and Lithuania progressed over the years gradually, and it was conditioned by the political situation in the country and the generosity of its rulers. Originally Jews in Lithuania enjoyed a considerable degree of religious and economic tolerance. They provided a useful service to the dukes and kings, who with insignificant exceptions, were benevolent and sympathetic to the plight of their Jewish subjects.

The above notwithstanding, in the middle ages the fortunes of the Jews of Vilnius were often affected by the constantly fluctuating political and economic conditions in the country, and their treatment was often a reaction to internal social pressures. Enraged by Jewish competition, and fearful for their own well-being, gentiles often blamed Jews for all their afflictions, and instigated anti-Jewish pogroms. In 1527 King Sigismund I granted a charter to the burghers of Vilnius which prohibited Jews from living and trading in the city.[4] Soon this charter was revoked, and in 1633 King Wladyslaw IV issued a new charter according to which Jews were allowed to reside in Vilnius and occupy themselves with commerce, trade, and crafts, but it also identified, for the first time, a special district where, ostensibly for their own safety and protection, Jews were advised to dwell.[5] Jewish residence, however, was not confined to this area only and gentiles were permitted to live in these so-called Jewish quarters as well.

Jewish life in Vilnius, however, was not free from internal pressures and discrimination. From time to time, the local administration would limit the freedom of its Jewish residents and introduce special legislation, forbidding Jews to reside in certain city districts or streets. Thus, in 1783 the local court ruled that Jews were forbidden to live on the street which led from the cathedral, located in the centre of the city, at the foot of the Castle Hill (Gedimino Pilis, Gora Zamkowa), to the Dawn Gateway (Ausros Vartai, Ostra Brama), a chapel which has become a Catholic shrine for it holds the famous sixteenth century image of the Virgin Mary. Jews were also not permitted to live on the street leading from the Traku Gates (Trocka Brama) to the St. John church. Ten years later the above restrictions were removed, and Jews were again permitted to dwell all over the city. On 10 September 1823, under Russian tsarist rule, the head of the Vilna police issued an order according to which the civil rights of the local Jews were again curtailed. This time the new regulation forbade Jews to live, lease, or conduct business on the main streets of the city, including Ostrobramska (Ausros Vartu), Zamkowa (Pilies), Swietojanska (St. John's), Dominikanska (Dominikonu), and Trocka (Traku). These restriction were not revoked until 1861.[6]

Over the years the Jewish community of Vilna grew and flour-
ished, and its educational institutions became famous all over Europe.
Many new settlers and immigrants from different towns, cities, and
countries were attracted by local Jewish scholars. Vilna was the home of
the Gaon - or eminence - Elijah ben Solomon (1720-1797), a man of
great intellectual prowess, highly versed in both Talmudic and secular
studies. Since early in the seventeenth century Vilna has become known
as the Jerusalem of Lithuania.

After the partition of the Polish-Lithuanian Kingdom the Jews of
Vilna lived under Russian tsarist rule, and most Jews in the city continued to reside in the cramped lodgings of the Jewish district, but despite
poverty and oppression Jewish life in Vilna was intense and vigorous. By
the middle of the nineteenth century Vilna was not only one of the
main centres of Yiddish and Hebrew secular and religious learning, but
also the hub of Jewish social and cultural activity in the diaspora.

For many years Vilna was the main point of concentration of Jewish political activity in Eastern and Central Europe, including both the
Zionist and the so-called Yiddishist movements. The Yiddishists were
mainly non-religious socialists, who supported the cause of Jewish workers. They opposed Zionism and recognized Yiddish, rather than Hebrew, as the national language of the Jewish people. The forerunners of
modern Zionism, members of *Hovevei Zion,* or lover of Zion, assembled
in Vilna in 1889. In 1902, the founding conference of the Zionist religious organization, *Mizrahi,* took place in the city. And in 1903 a conference of *Poalei Zion,* or the socialist Zionist party, gathered in the city.
Vilna was the cradle of Jewish socialism. In 1897 a socialist union of
Jewish workers, *Bund,* was established in Vilna. *Bund* was Yiddishist. It
protected the rights of Jewish workers, and assisted them in their struggle
with their Jewish employers.

After the First World war, under Polish rule, despite economic and
political difficulties Jewish life in the city continued to flourish, and
Wilno became , in a sense, the spiritual centre of the European Jewish
diaspora. Wilno was the home of the *YIVO*, the world famous Jewish
Scientific Research Institute, established in 1925. The main purpose of
the *YIVO* was to assist in the revival of the Jewish national conscious-
ness, and the investigation of current Jewish cultural, national, and intellectual problems. *YIVO* researchers placed special emphasis on the study

of the development of the Yiddish language and Yiddish linguistics.

Five Jewish publishing houses were active in the city, and six Yiddish and Hebrew newspapers appeared in the city regularly. Three Jewish public libraries, as well as a number of smaller book-lending institutions, were in operation. Among them was the famous Strashun Library, established in 1892, and named after the well known book collector Mathias Strashun (1817-1885) whose legacy, consisting of 7,000 rare volumes, formed the basis of the library's collection.

Before the Second World War intellectual and cultural life in Wilno was vibrant and many Jews were actively involved in fostering the development of literature, music, and the arts. The literary society *Yung Vilne* (Young Wilno), which listed among its members prominent writers and poets such as Ch. Grade, A. Sutskever, Sh. Kacherginski, and P. Miransky, was famous all over the world. An elaborate Jewish school network was in operation in the city, and there were elementary and secondary schools with Yiddish and Hebrew languages of instruction, as well as teachers seminaries for both Hebrew and Yiddish teachers. The Jewish community in Wilno was served by several Jewish professional theatres, many bands, choirs, and museums. For the faithful there were more than a hundred orthodox synagogues and houses of worship of different sizes, as well as religious schools and yeshivas. Best known was the so-called Great Synagogue, an imposing structure constructed in the seventeenth century, which could accommodate 3,000 worshippers. The Choral Synagogue, constructed in 1894, was the only one to survive both Nazi occupation and the onslaught of Soviet atheism.

Despite continuous squabbling between the Yiddishists and Zionists, between religious and secular Jews, as well as between different political parties within these movements, the Jewish Council of Wilno governed well Jewish communal life in the city, and took care of the old, handicapped , and the sick. Numerous Jewish charitable organizations and volunteers helped the poor. Jewish business organizations, professionals associations, and cultural, social, and political societies promoted Jewish interests, and inculcated their members with the skills necessary for survival in the complicated socio-political environment of pre-war Poland.

The invasion of Poland by the German Army, in September 1939, changed the fortunes of the Jews of Vilnius. The partition of Poland between Germany and the USSR divided the spheres of influence in Eastern Europe and, after a short interlude of Soviet rule, Vilnius was transferred, in October 1939, to Lithuanian jurisdiction, becoming again, after many years, the capital of independent Lithuania. That was when approximately 15,000 Polish Jews who managed to escape the Nazi onslaught turned up as refugees in Vilnius.

In the summer of 1940, under Soviet pressure, Lithuania agreed "voluntarily" to join the USSR. The incorporation of Lithuania into the Soviet Union had far reaching consequences for the Jews of Vilnius. Many, in particular simple working people, were happy with their newly acquired freedom and equality, and the alleged security provided by the virtue of becoming citizens of a powerful state such as the Soviet Union. But their hopes were short lived and they were able to enjoy these benefits only for a short while. Soon all forms of of Jewish political, religious, and national expression were suppressed or banned all together. All Zionist societies were dissolved, and the activity of the *Bund* was prohibited. Jewish religious education and the teaching of Hebrew were forbidden. Moreover, in June 1941, a week before the Nazi invasion of the USSR, many Jewish community leaders, political activists, business people, and intellectuals were arrested and exiled to Siberia.

The Nazi assault of the USSR, on 22 June 1941, and the capture of Vilnius two days later, stopped the Soviet purges, but it wiped out Jewish existence in the city altogether, and completely destroyed its bustling cultural, religious, and intellectual life.

Historically the size of the Jewish community of Vilnius was affected by economic and political conditions, but it basically grew with the general growth of the city. Before the Second World War, the Jews of Wilno constituted, at various times, between twenty five and fifty per cent of the total city population. Before the beginning of the First World War in 1914 the number of Jews in the city was the highest ever. It reached the total of 98,700.

Vilnius was liberated from Nazi occupation on 13 July 1944. In August 1944 a roll of the city population was taken, and some 600 Jews registered. It was assumed, at that time, that close to 500 Jews failed to disclose their real identity. However, only half of those registered were former residents of Vilnius, the others were Soviet born Jews who arrived in the city with the new Soviet administration from the USSR, as well as surviving Jews from other cities and towns in Lithuania. After the war, under Soviet rule, the Jewish population of Vilnius grew by the influx of residents from the Soviet Union, and it reached its highest level in 1959. The total population of Vilnius was then 236,078, including 16,534 Jews. Today, there are in Vilnius, the capital of independent Lithuania, close to 600,000 inhabitants, but only less than 4,000 Jews still continue to dwell in the city

The Nazi invasion of the Soviet Union started 22 June 1941. Two days later Vilnius was in the hands of the *Wehrmacht*. Soon after the German army entered Vilnius, the SS, the Gestapo, and the German civil administration made their appearance in the city, and the anti-Jewish atrocities began. A number of decrees, issued by the Germans, imposed numerous restriction on the Jews of Vilnius. Their objective was to intimidate and degrade the Jewish people, weaken their spirit, and dull their instincts of self-preservation. Moreover, by keeping them confused, and in the dark about their future, they wanted to turn them into easy prey for the Nazi death machine. Jews were ordered to turn in their telephones and radios, they were forbidden to have contacts with non-Jews, to sell their possessions, visit market places or use public transportation, parks, and recreational facilities. They were disallowed to walk on side walks and were required to march only in a single line on the right side of the road. All Jewish business and social activity was stopped, and a curfew from dusk to dawn was established for all Jews.

On 13 August 1941 Heinrich Lohse, the *Reichskommissar for Ostland*, issued a Provisional Directive the purpose of which was to introduce uniformity in the treatment of Jews all over occupied Eastern Europe. According to this Directive all Jews in *Ostland* were required "to identify themselves by wearing constantly visible yellow-six cornered stars, at least 10 CMS across, on the left side of the chest and in the centre of the back." Jews were also forbidden to attend schools of any type, attend theatres, movie houses, libraries or museums. The property of the Jews was to be confiscated and Jews were supposed to surrender immediately all local and foreign currency, securities, valuables of any kind, such as coins, gold and silver bullion, precious metals, jewellery, and precious stones in their possession. The same directives stated that the countryside was to be cleansed of Jews, and that ghettos were to be established in the cities where the number of Jews warranted it. The Jews were prohibited from leaving the ghettos, and the Jewish police in the ghettos was to be identified by wearing white armbands with a yellow star on the right upper arm.[7] A few days later a new regulation by *Reichsleiter* Alfred Rosenberg was made public. It ordered that all male and female Jews, of the ages between fourteen and sixty, were to be conscripted to forced labour.[8]

30 June 1941 the Lithuanian temporary Government announced the formation of auxiliary police battalions, the main objective of which was to assist the Nazis in their anti-Jewish endeavours, which involved mainly the rounding up and killing unsuspecting Jews. The murder of thousands of innocent Jews was something that in ordinary circumstances no normal human imagination could conceive. It was something no Jew in Vilnius wanted to believe. And yet, early in July 1941, when most Jews still refused to believe that German soldiers and Lithuanian policemen would be capable of indiscriminate murder, the Ponary (Paneriai) forest, just outside the city boundaries, was already turned into a place of mass murder and a grave for thousands of Jews, who with many other non-Jewish individuals, were the first to fall prey to the insatiable murderous Nazis.

"The systematic extermination of the Jews of Vilna started... when *Einsatzkommand 9* arrived and began its activities."[9] It appeared in the city 2 July 1941, and the massacres began a few days later. But individual Jews were indiscriminately murdered by the SS and the Lithuanian auxiliary police even earlier. The arrest of Jews in Vilnius began on the second day after the city was occupied by the Germans. 11 July 1941 was the day when the first Nazi victims were murdered in Ponary. 348 Jews and Soviet war prisoners, previously incarcerated in the Lukiszki prison were brought to Ponary for execution.[10]

The *Einsatzgruppe* "A" was composed of an operational squad (*Einsatzkommando*) and a special squad (*Sonderkommando*). The group "A" operational squad was commanded by the SS *Standartfuhrer* K. Jaeger, who on 2 July 1941 became also the head of Lithuanian security police. Immediately after the capture of Vilnius the Lithuanian local police and military units were placed under direct German command, and they became actively involved in the persecution of the local population, mainly the Jews. In June and July 1941 other German operational squads also made their appearance in Vilnius and by 8 July 1941 they murdered 321 Jews.

At the same time a special squad, *Ypatingas Burys (Sonderkommando)*, composed of close to a hundred of young armed Lithuanian thugs, was organized by the local authorities. At the beginning *Ypatingas Burys* was headed by the Lithuanian officer Juozas Sidlauskas. In November 1941 Lieutenant Balys Norvaisa became the leader of this special squad.[11] The members of the *Ypatingas Burys*, dubbed "chapunes" or "catchers," were roaming the streets of the city apprehending and leading away their young Jewish male victims. Those detained were never seen alive again. First they were taken to the Lukiszki prison, and later transferred to Ponary for execution. Since most of those captured were young males it was assumed, at first, that they were taken away somewhere for work. It did not take long, however, before rumours about Ponary began to spread and the horrid truth that all those detained by the so-called "chapunes" were murdered in cold blood became reality. In July and August 1941 the "catchers" murdered in Ponary on average some 500 Jews daily.[12] In total, members of this squad killed by 25 November 1941 18,898 people in Ponary, and another 13,501 in small towns in the Vilnius region. The absolute majority of those murdered were Jewish, but there were also some Soviet war prisoners and non-Jewish communists.[13]

The selective murder of Jews, conducted by the *Einsatzgruppen* and their local Lithuanian mercenaries, continued in Vilnius until the ghetto was established. By that time there was not a single Jewish family in the city that had not already lost, in these early months of occupation, some of its members to the hateful Nazi occupiers. From the approximately 80,000 Jews residing in Vilnius before the war, including thousands of Jewish refugees from Poland, about 35,000 were killed before the ghetto was established.[14]

The process of the creation of a ghetto varied from place to place, and in different locations ghettos were of different form and shape. In some instances ghettos were located on the outskirts of a town and enclosed with a wooden fence and barbed wire. When a ghetto was located in a central city district, inhabited mostly by Jews, the few gentiles residing there were usually resettled before the creation of the ghetto, and all other Jews in the city were transferred to the newly created ghetto. In this case windows in apartment buildings, and streets facing the outside of the ghetto, were bricked up, and in all instances the exit from, and entrance to, the ghetto were possible only through one gate constantly guarded by German soldiers and local policemen.

The local authorities in Vilnius began discussing the problems connected with the creation of a ghetto soon after the Germans captured the city. Already on the 30th of June 1941, a week after the Germans had appeared in town, a commission was formed that worked on the question of appointing a place to settle the Jews . On 18 July 1941 K. Kalendra (the manager of internal affairs of the Vilnius city and district municipal committee) reported to the Vilnius municipal committee about the technical preparation of the Jewish quarters (ghetto)…. "At the present time 10,224 people live in the quarters selected for the ghetto, and 78 per cent of them are Jewish. The ghetto is intended for 20,000 Jews, and all others are to be removed from the Vilnius district"[15]

Initially, it was indeed contemplated the creation of a ghetto for the 20,000 Jews, who were to remain in the city after the ghetto was established. It took, however, a while before a final decision about the location for the ghetto was reached. Some suggested that the ghetto be established in one of the suburbs. Others recommended that all Jews be resettled in a former military camp. The possibility of the creation of a ghetto for the Jews of Vilnius in one of the small towns in the vicinity of Vilnius was also considered. Late in August 1941, the Vilnius *Gebietskommissar*, Hingst, received an order from Heinrich Lohse, the head of the *Ostland Kommissariat*, to establish the ghetto in Vilnius in the part of the city where, at the given time, most Jews were residing. The German administration was obviously fed up with the indecisiveness of the local city authorities and ordered that the ghetto be created without delay in the so-called Old Town. Franz Murer, the German official in charge of Jewish affairs in the office of the *Gebietskommissar*, and the Lithuanian mayor of Vilnius, K. Dabulevicius, were charged with the final selection of the ghetto location.

The process of formation of the ghetto in Vilnius exhibited the hideous nature of the Nazis. On 1 September 1941 a proclamation, signed by Hingst, was posted all over the city. It stated that a day before "shots were directed from an ambush at German soldiers in Wilna. Two of the cowardly bandits were identified - they were Jews. To avoid such hostile acts in the future, new and severe deterrent measures were taken. The responsibility lies with the entire Jewish community. All Jews, men and women, are forbidden to leave their homes from today at 3 o'clock in the afternoon until 10 o'clock in the morning."[16] All that, of course, was a fiction fabricated by the Nazis and a provocation, but it had a purpose.

The special security measures announced by Hingst involved the eviction of all Jewish inhabitants from the areas designated for the ghetto. Indeed, on 31 August - 2 September 1941 all Jews who lived in the Old Town, men, women, and children, were forcefully driven to Lukiszki prison. On 1-3 September 1941 they were all transferred to the Ponary forest where they were indiscriminately slaughtered and buried in pits prepared for them in advance. After the district designated for the ghetto was emptied of its original Jewish inhabitants, the few gentile families residing there were moved to other parts of the city. Beginning at 6 A.M. on 6 September 1941, eleven weeks after the German army entered the city, all the Jews of Vilnius, who managed to survive the initial massacre, were driven into the narrow streets of the old Jewish quarters which were to become the newly created ghetto. By 7 P.M. on 7 September 1941 all Jews of the city were confined to this new communal prison.

Initially there were two ghettos in Vilnius, one on each side of Vokeciu (Niemiecka, Muzejaus) Street. This street was an important thoroughfare and it was kept open to regular city traffic. The large, first ghetto, was situated in the square between Vokeciu, Arkliu (Konska), Pylimo (Zawalna), and Lydos (Lidska) streets. The smaller, second ghetto, was composed of Zydu (Zydowska), Stikliu (Szkliana), Antokolskio (Antokolskiego), and Gaono (Gaona) streets. It included also the courtyard in which the Great Synagogue, and many small houses of worship were located. The creation of two ghettos was a shrewd Nazi ploy. It splintered the Jewish community, broke off lines of communication and made it easier to carry out the wicked Nazi plans.

The first few months in the ghetto were the most difficult ones. Indeed, young males were no longer assaulted daily by the so-called "catchers", but there were numerous other extermination actions which reduced the number of Jews in the ghetto by thousands. In addition, it took time to get settled in the new conditions of cramped ghetto life, secure proper employment, and procure the necessary means for physical survival.

Jews forcefully isolated in ghettos experienced their incarceration and Nazi atrocities in shock and disbelief. They were, however,

inadequately prepared by their life experience to be able to cope successfully with this new reality. In order to make Jews in the ghetto com-
pliant, fearful, and hard working, the Nazis placed them in conditions of
extreme tension and mental and physical stress. The exhaustive and
depressing living conditions, created by the Nazis, were combined with
deception and fraud which helped to divert the attention of the Jews
from imminent danger. The Jews in the ghetto were kept in the dark
about their future, and initially had no notion of the so-called "Final
Solution." The Nazis applied different means of disinformation and
psychological distraction in order to render the Jews helpless in the face
of a surprising attack, at the least probable time. By subjugating the Jews
to constant humiliation and degradation, by limiting their mobility and
access to information the Nazis intended to strip each Jew of his or her
self-esteem and destroy one's internal adaptive and defensive mechanism. Physical and mental torture were means of breaking resistance
and turning Jews into docile submissive victims.

From the first day of Nazi occupation the Jew was confronted
with a myriad of physical, social, and emotional dilemmas uncommon
to any individual in civilized society. Hence, daily existence was, first of
all, guided by the instinct of self- preservation and the struggle for physical
survival which was closely associated with the daily process of adapta-
tion to these new inhuman living conditions.

In ghetto conditions of extreme hardship the first step to survival
was recognition of the imminent danger of physical annihilation. The
denial of reality is usually a primitive psychological mechanism and, in a
sense, an expression of readiness to submit. In fact the first to perish,
under Nazi occupation, were those who had little faith in themselves,
but believed that it was someone else's duty to save them.

Since the ghetto was a social organization it was natural that it was
modelled on social structures in a free society. Yet the shape, form, and
activities of ghetto administrative bodies were usually determined by the
wishes of the oppressor. They were also influenced by the life experience and inclinations of those who were put in charge of these new
communal organizations.

The so-called Judenrat, or Jewish Council, was usually in charge of
the internal affairs in the ghetto. But the Judenrat was different from the
pre-war Jewish Communal Council. Its membership was not demo-

cratically elected, but rather appointed by the German administration. The Jewish Council was created by an immoral and vicious power and it functioned within a system of terror. It was set up by the Germans for one and only purpose, namely that German objectives be realized and their orders carried out with dispatch. The Judenrat created within the Jewish community an illusion of autonomy, but it was powerless when dealing with the German authorities. The administrative, economic, and cultural activities of the Judenrat were of no significance to the Germans, but they did not discourage any, because they helped to nurture illusions among the ghetto Jews and to conceal from them, for the time being, the already decided "Final Solution."

Since the members of Judenrats were Jewish, in the eyes of the Germans, they were potential future victims just as all other ghetto residents. Many Jewish communal leaders and rabbis in Vilnius were murdered in the early days of Nazi occupation, yet most ghetto Judenrat members, with the exception of some refugees from Poland and former residents of Lithuania, were people of long standing in civic life in pre-war Vilnius and were well known within the local Jewish community. Most members of the Judenrat were forced by the Nazis to accept their positions in the ghetto administration, and they certainly had good intentions. It was obvious that the paths to the death camps were not of their making. In the meantime, however, they have unwittingly become tools which the Nazis used to assist them in the realization of their murderous plans.

The Jewish councils tried hard, and used a variety of means, to postpone disasters, such as mass deportation and early ghetto liquidation, or failing that to reduce the extent of damage. At first, Judenrat leaders tried to negotiate with, and bribe, the local German rulers. Then, they sought ways to create work projects useful to the Nazis, and appealed to the Jews not to provoke the Germans. These Judenrat production designs were to justify the existence of the ghetto, and to illustrate to the Nazis that Jewish labour and its contribution to the German war economy was indispensable. In cases when deportation from the ghetto was inevitable Jewish leaders were most often prepared to assist in the selection of victims, with the purpose of sacrificing those individuals who, in their view, were at a given time most disposable, in order to save the majority.

In Vilnius the first Judenrat was appointed soon after the arrival
of the *Wehrmacht* in the city, several months before the ghetto was created. Initially it was composed of nine people. It did not take long before the Germans decided to increase the size of the Judenrat. According to an order of the German Field Commander, of 23 July 1941, a
new Judenrat composed of twenty-four members was to be created. It
included, among others, Dr. Jakob Vigodsky, Anatole Fried, Gregory
Jashunski, Leizer Kruk, and Dr. Naftali Margolis, all well known and
respected members of the pre-war Jewish community of Vilnius.[17]

Since Jewish resident in Vilnius were still scattered then all over the
city, and all lines of communication in the Jewish community were
shattered by anti-Jewish Nazi laws, the Judenrat was created not with the
purpose of supervising, coordinating , and administerting Jewish life in
the city, but with the intent of intimidating the Jews and extorting from
them all currency, gold, jewellery and valuables still in their possession.
Indeed, on 6 July 1941, several days after the first Judenrat was created,
Franz Murer, from the office of the *Gebietskommissar,* demanded that
within twenty-four hours the Judenrat delivers a penal contribution in
the amount of five million rubles (ten rubles, at that time, equalled one
Reichsmark). The Judenrat did not manage to collect and deliver the
money required and two of its members were killed. Most other members of the first Judenrat were murdered during the so-called "great
provocation," or the action before the creation of the ghetto, when the
residents of streets designated for the ghetto were murdered en masse.

Anatole Fried, a member of the first Judenrat, survived the massacre of the "great provocation" by hiding on the premises of the Jewish
hospital. On 7 September 1941, the day the ghetto was formed, Franz
Murer arrived in the ghetto, sought out Anatole Fried, and appointed
him chairman of the new Judenrat. Fried, in turn, nominated Jacob Gens,
who before the ghetto was acting superintendent of the Jewish hospital, to be chief of the ghetto police. The Germans approved the appointment. This initial Judenrat in the Vilnius ghetto functioned under
the leadership of Fried until 11 July 1942. Then it was formally dissolved by the Germans because they claimed that it was allegedly un-
productive, superfluous, and a waste of time. The Chief of the Ghetto
Police, Jacob Gens, was then appointed by the Germans as ruler of the
ghetto, officially "ghetto representative." Gens in turn appointed Fried

to the position of Director of ghetto administration, and Salek Desler as the new head of the ghetto police.

The fiction of Judenrat government in the Vilnius ghetto was ended already several months prior to this official change. "On 22 April 1942 Murer issued an order 1) That Police Chief Gens was given full responsibility for the ghetto 2) His police were to maintain order in the ghetto, execute directions of the regional Commissar, and see that work brigades marched off in columns 3) The watchmen at the gate were not to allow the importation of food into the ghetto 4) The police chief was warned that failure to comply with German commands meant his death."[18]

The creation of two ghettos in Vilnius and the removal of all Jews from the comfort of their own homes, in order to resettle them in the cramped conditions of the new quarters, hardly conducive for normal existence, uncovered the cunning nature of the oppressor. The intention was to unnerve the victims, place them in unfamiliar surroundings, and undermine their possible resolve to escape or resist. Initially the two ghettos in Vilnius were occupied by close to 40,000 Jews. 29,000 residing in the first ghetto, and 11,000 in the second.

It did not take long, however, before the real intentions of the Nazis to reduce the ghetto population became clear. The Jews hardly managed to settle in their new dwellings in the ghetto when the onslaught began. 1-2 October 1941, on the day of Atonement, during the so-called "Yom Kippur" action, 2,200 Jews from the first ghetto, and 1,700 from the second, were taken to Ponary for extermination. The following two days another 2,000 Jews were removed from the second ghetto and murdered in Ponary. Two weeks later, 15-16 October 1941, 3,000 residents of the second ghetto were transferred to Ponary and killed the same day. By the last week of October 1941 the second ghetto was virtually empty. For all practical purposes only one ghetto remained in the city. It appeared, however, that the Nazis still entertained some plans for the second ghetto and retained it for a while empty, but intact.

In the last week of October 1941 the German administration issued, on behalf of appropriate German employers, 3,000 special work permits, or the so-called "yellow certificates," to selected residents of the first ghetto. According to Nazi intentions there were to remain in the ghetto no more than 12,000 Jews, just enough to serve the local military and economic needs of the occupiers. This number included those who were actually employed by the Germans, as well as their family members composed of a spouse and no more than two children under sixteen. 24 October 1941, those with yellow passes went to work together with their families. In their absence all those remaining in the ghetto were removed for execution. 3 November 1941, holders of yellow certificates, and their families, were transferred to the vacated premises of the second ghetto. The first ghetto was then searched again for those in hiding. Three days later those with yellow certificates and their families were permitted to return from the second ghetto to their initial residences in the first ghetto. In the two actions, connected with the yellow passes, 6,200 Jews were rounded up and moved to Ponary for destruction. After having served the treacherous purpose of the Nazis the second ghetto was liquidates altogether.

It was well known in the ghetto that after the yellow certificate actions the actual ghetto population still exceeded the number allowed by the occupiers by many thousands. Among the illegal ghetto residents were Jews without yellow passes who managed to escape during the Nazi actions into temporary hiding places in the city, only to return back into the ghetto when the danger was over. There were also those who were able to delude the vigilant eye of the oppressor by concealing their existence in elaborate bunkers constructed well in advance in the ghetto. By November 1941, when the destructive actions ceased temporarily, and some stability was established, the ghetto was inhabited by close to 20,000 Jews. By then more then two thirds of the pre-war Jewish population of Vilnius had been brutally killed and buried in mass graves on the outskirts of the city. That did not mean, however, that the future of the ghetto was secure. The Head of the German S.D., security police, "K. Jaeger, stated in a report to his superiors, on 1 December 1941, that in Vilnius remained alive only those Jews, and their families, who worked for the *Wehrmacht,* but that even they could be easily liquidated."[19]

The Vilnius ghetto operated on the same principles as did most other ghettos in major European cities. It was extremely overcrowded. Each resident of the ghetto was allotted no more than approximately 1.5 square metres of living space. Several unrelated families of different social, cultural, and religious backgrounds were usually herded together in one room. People slept on bunks or on the floor, and were deprived of any privacy in what was regarded as their private lodgings. Running water was available in most dwellings, but in the cold winter apartments were poorly heated, because of the shortage of wood or coal, and the water pipes would often freeze and burst.

There was no central sewer system in the ghetto, and seldom a functioning toilet in an apartment, and all ghetto dwellers were forced to attend to their natural needs in latrines located in the courtyards of the houses. Most of these lavatories, however, were usually out of service, causing serious sanitation problems to the ghetto administration. Most flats had wood burning stoves in the kitchens, but there was seldom any firewood to cook a meal. Most people made use of hot plates to warm up the food, but the electric current was so weak that it would take hours to boil a cup of water. Moreover, most of the time electricity was available only in the morning from 7.30 A.M. to 9.00 A.M., and in the evening after 9.00 P.M., much to late to cook dinner.

In some East European ghettos the residents were deprived of any contact with the outside world. Industrial enterprises were constructed within the ghettos and all able-bodied Jews were employed there on a daily basis. In other ghettos Jews worked in German military units and enterprises of major economic and military significance, located outside the ghetto. In Vilnius most able-bodied ghetto residents worked outside the ghetto, but there were also a number of industrial enterprises within the ghetto. They produced goods for internal consumption, as well as for the use of the German administration. People working there were spared the inevitability of facing daily hostile Nazis. They were, however, deprived of the opportunity to venture outside the ghetto and procure some additional food.

The Jews employed outside the ghetto marched to and from work in groups. An appointed Jewish foreman, or brigadier, as he was then called, was in charge of the group. He was responsible for the performance of the gang, and for any transgressions of its members. According to an order of the *Gebietskommissar*, of 5 November 1942, Jewish workers were required to leave the ghetto between 6 A.M. and 9 A.M. and return from work sometimes between 3 P.M. and 8 P.M. Jews were to walk to work in gangs of no less than ten people. If there were less than ten workers employed in a certain place a special permit was to be issued.[20]

Malnutrition was one of the major problems facing ghetto inhabitants, because the food provided by the occupiers was hardly adequate for mere physical existence. The local city administration would apportion every month a certain amount of food for the whole ghetto population, taking into consideration the number of Jews residing in the ghetto, at a given time. The Jewish ghetto administration, in turn, would reduce the quantity of food provided by taking a substantial part of it for distribution among members of the ghetto Jewish bureaucracy and the police as additional rations to their regular bread cards. Only then, after having secured from the Judenrat appropriate bread vouchers, ordinary ghetto Jews would receive their meagre food portions. In such circumstances the survival of each ghetto resident depended on the ability of a family member, upon his or her return from work in the city, to smuggle in some food into the ghetto. The family bread-winner's safe return from work was one of the main concerns of each ghetto household. It was, however, forbidden by law to bring into the ghetto anything from the outside. Any attempt to smuggle in some food, or firewood, above the established limits, was regarded as a major crime.

It was the task of the Jewish police to check whether Jews returning from work tried to smuggle in anything. Usually Jewish ghetto gate guard policemen turned a blind eye to those who tried to bring some food into the ghetto. Occasionally, Lithuanian policemen standing at the ghetto gate would search those entering and take away whatever they would find. In some instances, Gestapo officers would arrive unexpectedly and conduct a brutal search of all those returning from work. The searches were usually ferocious. Everything, including a piece of bread or a few potatoes, was taken away. In order to instill fear in the ghetto residents, the so-called "smugglers" were often beaten, arrested and taken away to the Lukiszki prison. From there they were usually transferred to Ponary for execution.

Existence in the ghetto was usually conditioned by outside forces over which Jews had no control, and individual life was moved by the natural impulse of self-preservation. Hence, no long range plans for any activity were possible and the main preoccupation of every Jew was with practical matters of day-to-day survival. By 1942, well informed and knowledgeable people in the ghetto were aware of the fact that all

Jews under German rule were condemned to death, and that only the defeat of Nazi Germany could save those not yet murdered by the Nazis. Hence, daily reality posed the brutal question which concerned everyone. It asked not who was to live and who was to die, but rather who will be killed first and who later. Deep in one's heart, however, every ghetto Jew hoped for a miracle. Everyone believed that survival was possible and tried to do everything, within his or her means, to postpone imminent destruction for as long as possible.

This hope was nourished by the illusive and self-serving philosophy of so-called "life for work." The Vilnius ghetto Jewish administration cultivated the notion that Jewish labour was indispensable, and Jewish tradesmen irreplaceable, and that as long as Jewish workers performed well in the service of the German war cause, the ghetto would remain intact. To the Germans, however, it was always clear that ideological and racist consideration were more important than economic significance.

As early as on 15 November 1941 *Reichskommissar for Ostland*, H. Lohse, sent a letter to the Ministry of Eastern Territories in Berlin, inquiring whether the demands of the *Wehrmacht* for skilled Jewish workers be ignored, and all Jews in *Ostland* be liquidated regardless. The reply was blunt and unequivocal. It stated that "in principle, economic consideration are not to be taken into account in the settlement of the problem."[21] The above notwithstanding, 1942 was the year when the notion of "life for work" prevailed in the ghetto. The inhabitants of the ghetto, lulled by the relative peace, were able to conduct an illusory semi-normal existence in the shadows of the invisible and constantly lurking death. In spite of all odds, and perhaps just because of it, life in the ghetto was an expression of boundless hope for survival and an extreme example of the will to live.

Despite the incredibly difficult living conditions in the ghetto, and the abiding danger of total annihilation, the ghetto in Vilnius operated as a well managed ostensible mini-state. The Judenrat organized a ghetto administration which was composed of a number of departments, concerned with different aspects of daily life, such as health, food, housing, labour, industry, social welfare, and culture among others. Each member of the Judenrat was responsible for the work and supervision of several departments and services. The health department was in charge of the hospital which by mid 1942 became a major health institution with 237 beds. The ghetto residents were also served by an out-patient clinic, an epidemiological sanitary programme, a disinfection centre, and a vaccination programme. Vitamins and medication production was established in the ghetto, and public health measures such as bathing and delousing became a part of regular ghetto existence. Bread cards were withheld from those who failed to provide evidence of a bath visit and disinfection. On average close to 300 patients were treated in the ghetto hospital monthly. At the same time, over fifty inpatients, and close to eighty outpatients, were given X-ray treatment, including diagnosis and therapy. In order to keep the Germans from knowing about the presence in the ghetto of patients with typhus, and other infectious diseases, the department of infectious diseases was called "observation department," and doctors officially diagnosed typhus as "feverish condition." The hospital pharmacy filled between seven and eight hundred prescriptions monthly. *Folksgezunt* (Public Health), a Yiddish journal on medicine and public health, published in pre-war Poland, continued to appear, from time to time, in the Vilnius ghetto in the form of a "living newspaper." Every two weeks lectures, announcements, and question and answer periods on medical topics were organized in the hall of the ghetto theatre. Transcripts of the meetings were posted at various points in the ghetto.[22]

The social welfare department provided the needy with different forms of assistance, such as food, cash, medical aid, payment of rent, and day care for children. Public kitchens operated by the department distributed hot meals to the needy free of charge, and tea houses provided them with boiled water on a steady basis. The department was also in charge of the orphanage in the ghetto, it assisted with the operation of the day-care centre, and distributed to the needy supplies which previously belonged to Jews deported by the Nazis.

The labour department was, in a sense, an employment office which supplied the German administration and *Wehrmacht* with the required number of specialist, tradesmen and labourers. At different times, between 1942 and September 1943, between eight and ten thousand ghetto Jews worked in the city, and close to 2,000 people were employed inside the ghetto. In order to satisfy the demand for tradesmen in the city special courses to train painters, carpenters, glaziers, and bricklayers were organized in the ghetto, and the technical school in the ghetto trained electricians, locksmiths, metal workers and plumbers. Originally Jewish workers in the city were paid by their employers and earned on average 300.00 rubles (30.00 Reichsmarks) a month. Late in 1942, depending on the qualifications of those employed, the pay of Jewish workers was somewhat raised, but the working day was extended from eight to ten hours daily. According to an order of the *Gebietskommissar*, of 5 November 1942, Jewish men of over sixteen were to be paid 0.15 Reichsmarks per hour; women of over sixteen 0.125 Reichsmarks per hour, and youths under sixteen 0.10 Reichsmarks per hour.[23] The money earned at work was a fraction of what was necessary for the mere survival of a family. Indeed, the price of one kilogram of bread inside the ghetto was, at different times, between thirty and eighty rubles.

The department of industry organized, and was in charge of, the workshops and factories established in the ghetto. These enterprises were mainly busy with filling orders from the *Wehrmacht* and German institutions, but they served also the internal needs of the ghetto population. There were in the ghetto metal workshops, furniture factories, a factory producing matrasses, a smelting plant, shoemaking and tailoring workshops, as well as enterprises producing medical instruments, dishes, vitamins, detergent, tooth paste, syrup, saccharin, lemonade, and candy.

The cultural needs of the ghetto population were served by a public library, a theatre, symphony orchestra, two choirs, a sport club, as well as children's and youth clubs. The Judenrat formed also a Jewish police, Jewish court, constructed a jail, and published a wall bulletin, *Geto yedies* (Ghetto News). There were in the ghetto several privately operated restaurants, coffee and tea houses, several general stores, a book store, a pawn shop, and even a clandestine bawdy house. The financial resources of the Judenrat were limited, but it charged ten per cent of income tax on the salaries of all working Jews. In addition, it had some profit from the operation of the workshops in the ghetto, and it collected payments for rent, medical services, bread cards, various fines, etc. There was in the ghetto also a home for the aged, and public kitchens for adults and children where, for a small fee, hot cooked meals were served daily.

The department of culture was primarily concerned with the work of the schools. There were in the ghetto two general elementary schools, one secondary school, and a music school. Education was compulsory in the ghetto for all children between the ages of five and thirteen. 2,700 children between the ages of seven and fourteen attended ghetto schools. A day-care centre and a children's nursery served the needs of working mothers. Working women could leave there their children from 7 A.M. to 6 P.M. and pick them up after their return from work.

The educational process in the ghetto schools was conducted according to curricula approved by the department of culture, and the political affiliation of the head of this department determined the subject matter and language of instruction in the ghetto schools. The ideological future of the ghetto children was always a bone of contention in the conflict between political adversaries in the ghetto, and the struggle between Zionists and Yiddishists, or those who supported Yiddish at the expense of Hebrew, in the ghetto schools was rampant. When the head of the department of culture was a Yiddishist the emphasis in school curricula was always on the Yiddish language and related subject. When a Zionist, however, would replace the Yiddishist as head of the department Hebrew would usually become the main language of instruction.

Religion was always an important part of Jewish life and education in pre-war Wilno. Before the war there were no Jewish conservative or reform congregations in the city, and all religious affiliation and worship was strictly orthodox. After the Nazis captured the city most religious leaders were murdered in the early anti-Jewish actions. In the ghetto conditions of slavery, when work was compulsory six days a week, it was difficult to observe Jewish religious rituals or dietary laws. At the same time, a variety of different notions questioning the role of Providence in the widespread murder of innocent Jews circulated in the ghetto. Some ghetto residents were even asserting that the Holocaust was a punishment for the sins of assimilation. Most Jews in the ghetto, however, refused to abandon their faith and, within their limited possibilities, conducted a Jewish traditional life. Three synagogues served the needs of the faithful, and a religious school as well as a small yeshiva functioned within the walls of the ghetto.

Despite the external appearance of a normal life, which could satisfy the curiosity of a detached Red-Cross observer, the ghetto system of government was a devilish invention of the Nazis. It was created with the purpose of deceiving the Jews. By providing those herded together within the ghetto walls with a false sense of security, the Nazis were able to perpetrate and facilitate their next act of mass murder. In fact, the hospital, the home for the aged, and the orphanage were turned, by the occupiers, into gathering stations for all those they regarded as dispensable. From time to time the Gestapo would arrive unexpectedly and remove from the ghetto the sick, homeless, and vulnerable for immediate destruction.

Similarly, the ghetto jail was not a comfortable nor secure place to stay. It was not a location where convicted criminals served time. It was rather a temporary, but dangerous, detention point. The Jewish ghetto police was required to submit regularly to the local authorities lists of Jews incarcerated in the ghetto jail, indicating their surnames, names, and reason for arrest.[24] It was well known in the ghetto that, from time to time, German security police would unexpectedly arrive, enter the prison through a special gate directly from the city and empty its premises. In many instances what might have appeared, at first, as a temporary detention turned into a death sentence since all those removed to Lukiszki were soon transferred to Ponary for execution.

The intensity of existence in the ghetto was so high that there was little time to reflect on the past. All one's thoughts were concerned with the present. Moreover, it was senseless to plan for the future. The difficult conditions of ghetto life forced Jews to master a variety of survival skills. Some connected with physical existence, others with mental and emotional well-being. The grief of loss of the near ones was usually muffled by the continuous danger to oneself, and those who were still alive.

Social life alleviated, in some measure, the sensation of pervading doom and pessimism. Social, cultural or political activity was, in a sense, a mode of mental and emotional escape and a form of spiritual resistance. It was also a means of defiance, an affirmation of one's existence, and a refusal to accept the inevitable. It raised young people in the ghetto, even if only temporarily, to the level of ordinary human beings. There were in the ghetto a number of youth groups, formed mostly by former school friends, political comrades, coworkers, and new acquaintances. The activity of these independent groups provided their members with an opportunity to spend time together, exchange opinions, and make new friends. Human contacts were extremely important in the ghetto. Jews worked in different military and private enterprises in the city. Daily they would come in touch with a variety of people and return home with an abundance of different kinds of information. This information, brought into the ghetto from the outside, circulated from mouth to mouth. It was extremely important to the Jews, because no radios, telephones, or newspapers were available in the ghetto. The ghetto resembled a huge gossip mill. Jews were particularly interested in, and sensitive to, any news about the situation at the eastern front, as well as information concerning the safety and future of the Jews in the Vilnius ghetto.

Most Jews in the ghetto lived a double life. On the job, outside the ghetto, they kept a low profile, tried to remain inconspicuous, and bide their time. Most tried to perform their duties well in order to find favour with their employers and not incur the wrath of those in charge. In fact, a Jewish worker was never out of danger. Any German or Lithuanian could accuse him or her of sabotage with all the consequences to follow. When after a long day of work, and a march on the road where horses and carts travel, the downtrodden Jew successfully passed the control at the gate and entered the ghetto he or she felt, all of a sudden, a certain relief and a sense of illusory freedom. This was, however, the freedom of degradation, the freedom of slavery. It was the freedom of an animal in a large cage, always at the mercy of his master. Once inside the ghetto it appeared to the Jew that, at least temporarily, he or she was free from the external pressures of an alien environment. In the ghetto, the Jew was an equal among his fallen brethren. He was not looked down upon, nor was he taunted by anyone. And above all he was with those who shared his destiny and wished him well. He was able to forget himself and, at least for a while, indulge in activities which provided him with an escape from his oppressive existence.

In order to divert the attention of the Jews from impending danger, the Germans permitted the establishment in the ghetto of a number of cultural, social, and recreational institutions which helped create a semblance of a normal existence. The ghetto theatre was located in the premises of the former so-called small city hall on 3 Konska (Arkliu) Street. Since Konska Street constituted one of the outside ghetto walls, the only available entrance to the theatre was through 6 Rudnicka

(Rudninku) Street. The hall contained 315 seats. The first performance of the theatre opened as scheduled on 18 January, 1942. During the first year of operation the theatre gave 111 performances, and sold 34,804 tickets.[25] Israel Segal, a pre-war Jewish actor from Kaunas and Siauliai, was the artistic director of the theatre. He attributed the initiative of founding a theatre in the ghetto to Jacob Gens. When the theatre celebrated its firs anniversary, Gens proudly assumed the responsibility of having established the theatre which produced also revue-variety programmes, all based on original material, written in the ghetto.

The ghetto symphony orchestra, conducted by Mr. W. Durmashkin, as well as Yiddish and Hebrew choirs and soloists performed, from time to time, in the same hall. In January 1943, on the first anniversary of the theatre, a festival of the arts was organized on the premises of the ghetto theatre. The programme included the reproduction of several plays staged earlier, recitals of musicians and singers, concerts of the ghetto choirs, the ghetto symphony orchestra, and the jazz ensemble. The last show, staged in August 1943, was interrupted by the liquidation of the ghetto.

Intellectual life in the ghetto did not stagnate. The professional intelligentsia looked for ways to continue the quest for mental stimulation. Various professional societies, such as an association of writers, musicians, and artists, an association of scientists, and a union of physicians and medical workers, were organized. These societies arranged regularly meetings, seminars, and public lectures, attended by its members as well as by representatives of the general public.

The ghetto sport club was at first located on 6 Strashun Street, next to the ghetto bath-house and jail. There were several ill-equipped gyms in the ghetto and a basketball court. The sport club was a place where young people would gather to train in gymnastics, rhythmics, running and jumping games, boxing, as well as basketball and volleyball. The sport club had a steady active membership of 415. But many more participated in the sport festivities organized by the club. In September 1942 ghetto championship in basketball and volleyball were conducted and sixteen and eighteen teams respectively took part in the competitions.[26] Occasionally special sport festivities were organized in the ghetto, and ghetto youngsters performed in the presence of Jewish ghetto leaders and German officers. Basketball competitions were conducted at 6 Strashun Street, while gymnastic exhibitions and boxing matches were organized in the ghetto theatre hall. It was not easy to exert oneself and perform in depressing ghetto condition, but the prizes, such as half a kilogram of sugar or butter, awarded at sport competitions were of great importance. Malnutrition and starvation were rampant in the ghetto, and a pound of butter could save a life.

It is evident from the above that even in the harrowing ghetto conditions, when the threat to one's physical survival was always real, the Jewish captives sought food for spiritual nourishment. Cultural, artistic, and political activity satisfied, at least partially, their thirst for enlightenment. It provided them also with an escape from the indignities of daily life, and nurtured the hope for a better future. It is necessary, however, to note that not all ghetto residents approved of organized recreational programmes such as music, theatre, or sport in the ghetto. They believed that in the shadows of the mass graves in Ponary the ghetto was no place for such activities. Herman Kruk, the ghetto historian and librarian, as well as a noted political figure in the ghetto, was one of those who conducted a campaign against opening the theatre. On 17 January 1942 Kruk wrote in his diary that "You do not play theatre in a graveyard."[27] The next day this slogan appeared in the form of graffiti on the walls in the ghetto. Gens threatened Kruk with punishment if he continued with his politics of resistance, and Kruk relented. Later Kruk changed his mind and stopped opposing cultural activity in the ghetto.

Gens believed that the normalization of life in the ghetto, and the increase in the productivity of its residents, may ensure the survival of a greater number of Jews in the ghetto. He considered the theatre to be not only a source of work and existence for the artists, but also a useful tool to heighten the spirit and morale of the ghetto Jews. Therefore, Gens urged the theatre to maintain its activity regularly. In fact, the second performance of the theatre took place one week after the first. This time without opposition. Herman Kruk noted in his diary that one could see among the guests at this performance the Nazi officer Herring, and a commander of the Lithuanian militia which participated in the executions in Ponary. The two, according to Kruk, came drunk, and left during the intermission.[28]

The ghetto library, located at 6 Strashun Street, opened its doors two days after the ghetto was established. Two weeks later, on 19 September 1941, in the middle of a bloody deportation action, 1,485 readers had been already registered in the library, and 400 books were being lent out daily. The library was always busy and short of books. Since there were no newspapers or radios in the ghetto, library books were in great demand. Reading fiction was a means of escaping into another, more beautiful, world. After every anti-Jewish action in the ghetto the number of readers would increase. The day after the 1 October 1941 "Yom Kippur" action, when several thousand Jews were driven away from the ghetto and shot in Ponary, 300 books were lent out by the library. In fact, books were signed out from the library until the very last day of the ghetto existence. On 13 October 1942 the ghetto library celebrated the lending of the 100,000[th] book. Out of the close to 17,000 ghetto inhabitants, 4,700 were library subscribers.[29] It is interesting to note that 70.4 per cent of all books taken out from the library in 1941-42 were in the Polish language, 19.4 per cent in Yiddish, and 1.3 per cent in Hebrew. 8.9 per cent were in other languages such as Russian, Lithuanian, and German.

That did not mean, of course, that the Nazis were indifferent to what the Jews in the ghetto were reading. To the contrary, along with physical destruction they were also intent on annihilating the Jewish cultural and religious heritage and obliterating everything connected with Jewish intellectual and spiritual life. Since Vilnius was recognized as one of the most important centres of Jewish learning it received special attention from the Nazi authorities.

In July 1941 Dr. Gothart, an adviser to Heinrich Himmler, arrived in Vilnius. He assembled a group of Jewish scholars and ordered them to segregate and prepare lists of all Jewish books of any academic and scholarly significance for transportation to Germany. In January 1942 Dr. Pohl, an adviser to *Reichsleiter* Alfred Rosenberg and the director of the Frankfurt Museum for the Study of East-European Peoples, appeared in the city. Delegated by the Nazis in 1933 for three years to Jerusalem to study Jewish literature and oriental studies, Dr. Pohl was consequently regarded by the Nazis as a leading specialist in Jewish affairs. Under his supervision the most important Jewish books from the famous Strashun library and the *YIVO* archives and library were sent to Germany, while most other books were sold for pulp, or simply destroyed. Only a fraction of the Jewish books, available in Vilnius before the war, were saved by the few Jews employed by Dr. Pohl's organization. They risked their lives daily in order to save the remnant of the Jewish cultural heritage.[30] Similarly, risking his own life Antanas Ulpis, the former head of the Lithuanian State Book Chamber, managed to save some of the *YIVO* materials in the days of Nazi occupation and Stalinist rule.

Even in the days of relative peace life in the ghetto was full of paradoxes and dangers of different kinds. Most ghetto residents were young or middle-aged, but even young and healthy people were getting ill, and the treatment of any serious illness could cause insurmountable difficulties. There was a severe shortage of medication for the treatment of even the simplest infection, and ghetto conditions, including malnutrition, were not conducive for the healing process and a speedy recovery of the sick. And yet, there were no outbreaks of epidemics or contagious diseases in the Vilnius ghetto and its streets were not covered with dead and emaciated bodies, as it was the case in some other ghettos in Poland. Moreover, general sanitation rules were strictly enforced by the ghetto administration, and any sign of dangerous illness was concealed from the Germans.

As in any other communal setting death from natural causes in the ghetto was a normal occurrence. The loss of a close family member is always perceived as a great tragedy. In those days, however, when great numbers of Jews were killed daily, and savage murder was as common to every Jew in the ghetto as life itself, many ghetto residents were envious of those who, rather then being slaughtered by raging Nazis and thrown into mass graves, died their own natural death and were taken for interment to the Vilnius Jewish cemetery. Those who died their own death in the ghetto were considered fortunate. They were looked upon as the ones chosen by God. Death from natural causes was, in a sense, an act of defiance and a victory over the Nazi system of mass murder. The Nazis could oppress, torment, and kill those who were alive, but they had no power over the dead.

The funeral procession in the ghetto would usually follow a horse driven cart with the casket. It could, however, proceed only up to the gates of the ghetto. No one except for the coachman and a worker were permitted to follow to the graveyard. The graves of those who died in the ghetto and buried at the Jewish cemetery were unmarked, but the Jewish religious community kept a record of the places and names of those who were buried there. It was hoped that in the future, after the downfall of the Nazi enemy, family members could erect a monument and commemorate appropriately the death of their deceased relative.

Paradoxically, there were few suicidal deaths in the ghetto. In normal circumstances people kill themselves when the terror of death becomes less horrifying then the horror of life, and inclinations of suicide appear when the complete exhaustion of love of life sets in. In 1941-1944, when Jews in Nazi occupied territories were often reduced to walking skeletons, the suicide rate among them actually declined by 65 per cent from the pre-war level.[31] These facts may be puzzling, but it appears that in the austere and cruel circumstances of Nazi tyranny life acquired new meaning. Life itself, expressed in the miracle of existence which is beyond human comprehension, gave meaning to suffering, and energy to cope and hope. In conditions of complete degradation and constant danger of destruction physical survival, and hope that the enemy will be vanquished, became the meaning of life.

The relative peace in the ghetto was often upset by the tidings from the surrounding towns and villages in the region. Residents of the ghetto could not ignore the disturbing news about the massacres taking place in the vicinity. These accounts shattered their false sense of security, and sharpened their awareness of the closeness of disaster. Many fugitives, from small towns in the vicinity of Vilnius, who managed to escape Nazi slaughter, had nowhere to hide and from time to time were turning up in the Vilnius ghetto. Stories about the heinous crimes perpetrated by the Germans, and their local collaborators, were spreading from mouth to mouth.

At one instance, in April 1943, the Germans duped thousands of Vilnius region small town inhabitants by assuring them that they will be transferred to the ghetto in Kaunas. Instead, they were taken to Ponary and murdered. Such disturbing news did little to assuage the uneasiness of the Jews in the Vilnius ghetto. To the contrary, they reminded them about their own vulnerability and the constantly lurking danger to their survival.

In the summer of 1943 the tension in the ghetto mounted, and the concern for its continuous existence heightened. The relative peace in the ghetto came to an abrupt end. In the middle of July 1943 it became clear in the ghetto that the Nazis were aware that some ghetto residents were involved in clandestine anti-Nazi activity, and that Yitzhak Witenberg, a Jew from the ghetto, was a members of the underground communist party committee in Vilnius. The ghetto Jewish administration believed, at that time, that the Germans were not aware of the fact that Witenberg was the leader of the F.P.O., (*Fareinikte partizaner organizatsie*) or the United Partisan Organization, a Jewish anti-Nazi underground resistance organization which operated clandestinely within the walls of the ghetto. The Jewish ghetto leaders were forced to agree to surrender Witenberg to the Nazis hoping that this sacrifice will save the ghetto inhabitants from serious repercussions. The leaders of the Jewish underground hesitantly accepted the same view. Time had proven them both wrong.

On 21 June 1943 the *Reichsfuhrer SS* Heinrich Himmler issued an order about the liquidation of the ghettos in *Ostland*. It stated: "1. I order that all Jews still remaining in ghettos in the *Ostland* area be collected in concentration camps. 2. I prohibit the withdrawal of Jews from concentration camps for (outside) work from August 1, 1943. 3.... The workshops are to be solely concentration camp workshops. 4. Inmates of the Jewish ghettos who are not required are to be evacuated to the east."[32] It is obvious today that according to Himmler's directive no ghettos were to remain in Nazi occupied Eastern Europe after 1 August 1943. It is also well known, however, that some ghettos, including the other two major ghettos in Lithuania, in Kaunas and Siauliai, were transformed into concentration camps and avoided immediate liquidation for another eight months.

The fate of the ghetto in Vilnius was different. Archival documents confirm today that the liquidation of the ghetto in Vilnius was hastened by the German realization of the existing connection between the communist underground in the city and the underground movement in the ghetto, as well as by the possibility of armed resistance within the ghetto.[33] In fact, the Germans were aware that a Jewish anti-Nazi resistance organization existed in the Kaunas ghetto as well. The Kaunas ghetto, however, was located in a secluded part of the city and it would be easy to destroy it anytime without German casualties. In Vilnius the situation was different. The ghetto was in the centre of the city, and an uprising in the ghetto would create havoc in the city. Moreover, it would last long and require the involvement of major German military forces. Hence, the Witenberg affair, and the realization that there were armed Jews in the ghetto, obviously precipitated the Nazi resolve to liquidate the ghetto in Vilnius without delay. This decision was further reinforced by the arrest in the city of a number of Jews who were trying to buy guns from gentiles, and smuggle them into the ghetto. In addition there were instances when not far from the city groups of armed young Jews, that were on their way to the forest to join the partisans, were ambushed by German military units.

By early August 1943 the situation crystalized and it became evident that the future of the ghetto was in doubt. On 6 August 1943 the Germans started to round up Jews without warning for transportation to concentration camps in Estonia. Two weeks later, 19-24 August 1943, Jews from the ghetto were abducted again, and another consignment of prisoners was shipped to Estonia. The above notwithstanding the Germans promised that the remaining Jews in the ghetto will continue to live and work safely as before. That was, of course, another sham. The ghetto administration, as well as the leadership of the underground resistance movement, hesitantly believed the Germans and hoped that another period of tranquillity in the ghetto will begin, and life will go on without much change. Soon, however, on 1 September 1943, the abduction of ghetto residents for transportation to Estonia resumed with new force, and without advance notice. From that day on, Jews were no longer permitted to go to work outside the ghetto.

Between 6 August and 5 September 1943 some 7,130 Jews were deported to Estonia, and in the ghetto remained no more than between 11,000 and 12,000 residents. In the morning of 5 September 1943 the German security officer, in charge of Jewish affairs, Bruno Kittel, arrived in the ghetto and delivered a new means of chicanery. He told Gens that the Jews of Vilnius had been given a new lease of life, and that the *Wehrmacht* had placed an order for thousands of overcoats and felt boots to be produced in the new workshops to be established in the ghetto. The Germans intended, of course, to deceive the Jews once more and by providing them with false hopes discourage any attempts of resistance or escape. A week later several thousand qualified workers were moved from the ghetto to the *Herres Kraft Park* (H.K.P.) and *Kailis* labour blocks in the city, while some others were sent to live and work at the German military hospital and at the offices of the German security police. Thus there were no more than approximately 9,000 Jews remaining in the ghetto.[34]

The ghetto in Vilnius survived for two years. Its final liquidation began on Thursday, 23 September 1943. The Germans announced that the ghetto will be liquidated and that all its inhabitants will be sent to a labour camp in Estonia. That was another lie. In fact, men and women were separated, and close to 2000 healthy men were sent to Estonia. Some 1500 young women were sent to the Kaiserwald labour camp, near Riga, in Latvia. The remaining women and children were transported to death camps for immediate destruction, and several hundred elderly and sick were murdered in Ponary. It is necessary to note, however, that most middle-aged man and women were marked for immediate extermination. In those days, in conditions of extreme oppression and suffering, people aged quickly. Any teenager was regarded as a mature individual, and those over forty were considered elderly and decrepit.

According to a statement of the German Security Police and SD in Vilnius, dated 11 November 1943, there were before in ghettos and concentration camps in the district of Vilnius 24,108 Jews. Until 11 November 1943 8,019 were killed, 14,000 were transferred to Estonia, and 2,382 Jews were still left over in the city. In the countryside there were still remaining some 1,720 Jews.[35]

Several thousands Jewish specialists in Vilnius escaped execution for another eights months. These were the workers who lived all the time in two special blocks outside the perimeters of the ghetto. One group was employed in the fur and leather manufacturing plant, *Kailis*, another group, consisting of mechanics and engineers, was employed by the German company *Herres Kraft Park* (H.K.P.), and was engaged in the repair of military vehicles and other combat equipment. Most residents of *Kailis* and H.K.P., however, did not survive the war. A week before the liberation of Vilnius from Nazi occupation these special blocks were transferred from the *Wehrmacht* to the SS and their residents were taken to Ponary for execution. Those who tried to resist, or escape, were killed on the spot. Except for the few who managed to evade detection in hiding, the Germans killed all others just several days before the Soviet Army entered Vilnius.

Late in 1943, in anticipation of the possible withdrawal from Vilnius, the Nazis devised a plan the intention of which was to cover up all traces of their crimes. With that purpose they brought eighty Jews and Soviet war prisoners to Ponary, and keeping them literally in chains, the Nazis forced them to exhume the corpses of the victims murdered there and cremate them on the spot. According to various accounts, between December 1943 and 15 April 1944, between 56,000 and 68,000 corpses were exhumed and burned in Ponary. The night of 15 April 1944 thirteen of the slave labourers managed to escape from their dungeon in Ponary. Eleven of them joined the anti-Nazi partisans in the Rudninku forest (Rudnicka puszcza). [36]

Poster (in Yiddish) announcing about the performances, in January, 1943, of the Jewish ghetto theatre, the jazz band, the Yiddish choir, and the musical ensemble.

Poster (in Yiddish) announcing about a literary-musical evening to take place 6 March 1943, at the premises of the Jewish ghetto theatre.

SPORT ACTIVITIES IN THE VILNIUS GHETTO

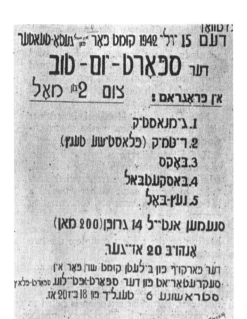

Poster (in Yiddish) announcing about sport festivities to take place, on 15 July 1942, at the premises of the Jewish ghetto theatre. The program included: gymnastics, rythmics, boxing, basketball, and volley-ball.

August 1942. Sport competitions, in the presence of the Jewish ghetto leaders, at the playground of 6 Strashun Street. Sitting in the first row: fourth from the left is the ghetto police Chief, S. Desler, sixt from the left is the Head of the ghetto Jacob Gens.

THE FIRST GHETTO IN VILNIUS
CURRENT LOCATION

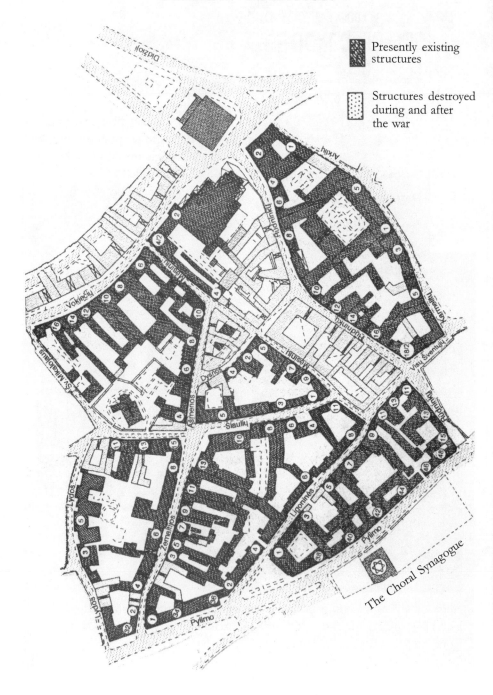

Presently existing structures

Structures destroyed during and after the war

The Choral Synagogue

CHAPTER TWO:
Yitzhak Witenberg and the F.P.O.

Yitzhak Witenberg

Yitzhak Witenberg and the F.P.O.

THE NAME OF YITZHAK WITENBERG IS INexorably linked with the history of the F.P.O. *Fareinikte Partizaner Organizatsie*, or the United Partisan Organization, in the Vilnius ghetto. It is also closely connected with the anti-Nazi communist underground movement in Lithuania, especially in the city of Vilnius. In both organization Witenberg played a prominent role. His life experience prepared him, albeit with some failings, for this important task.

Witenberg was born in Vilna in 1907 into a working class family. He received his basic education in a Yiddish language primary school and went on to learn the leather dressing and fur trade. After the First World War, the life of Jewish workers in Wilno (Poland) was not easy, and many became active in the revolutionary labour movement. Early in his life Witenberg became involved in trade union activity, and in 1936 he was elected to the position of Chairman of the Leather Workers Trade Union in Wilno, becoming concurrently a member of the Council of Trade Unions in the city of Wilno. At the same time, Witenberg combined his work in trade union organizations in Wilno with clandestine communist political activity, and he joined the local branch of the illegal Polish Communist Party. This was a daring and risky undertaking, because all communist in Poland were arrested, and often kept in prison for many years without trial.

In September 1939, after the invasion of Poland by Germany, Wilno was occupied by the Red Army. By the end of October 1939 the Soviets transferred the city and vicinity to Lithuanian jurisdiction. Witenberg, the communist, preferred to live in the Soviet Union, rather than in capitalist Lithuania, and he moved eastwards together with the retreating Red Army. He settled then in Dokszyc, before the war a town in North-Eastern Poland, but currently a part of Soviet Western Belorussia. In Dokszyc Witenberg became again involved in political and cultural activity.[1]

In 1940, when independent Lithuania was forced to join "voluntarily" the Soviet Union, Witenberg returned to Wilno, now renamed to Vilnius the capital of Soviet Lithuania. He resumed his trade union activity, and was reappointed to his old post of chairman of the leather workers trade union. In June 1941, when Germany invaded the USSR, Witenberg tried to escape the Nazi onslaught by evacuating together with other Soviet bureaucrats deep into the Soviet hinterland. The German army, however, moved faster eastward than the remnants of the Soviet administration, and Witenberg, with many other former Soviet officials, remained behind in the territories occupied by the Germans.

Under Nazi rule, even before the ghetto was established, Witenberg was forced to go into hiding. After the ghetto was created he did not dare go to work in the city, because he could easily be recognized as a former communist activist and betrayed by his enemies to the Gestapo. Thus, he sought work inside the ghetto and was employed at the epidemiological-sanitation department of the ghetto administration. At one time he worked in the ghetto bath, and was assigned the job of checking admission tickets of those arriving to bathe.

According to the lists of ghetto prisoners, compiled during the may 1942 census in Lithuania, Witenberg lived with his family in the ghetto at 11 Strashun Street, Apt. 13. The apartment was occupied by five families and four single individuals, in total twenty-one people. Witenberg's family was composed of four. His wife Riwa was born in 1901, his older son Hirsh was born in 1927, and his younger son Moishe in 1930. 1906 is indicated as Witenberg's year of birth.[2] It is necessary, however, to point out that the ghetto census lists were not always accurate, because without original documents Jews in the ghetto were often able to change their names and birth dates in order to make them conform with the requirements of German labour permits.

In the ghetto Witenberg did not give up his involvement in political activity, and the idea of armed resistance to the Nazi occupiers became the guiding torch of all his endeavours. He started by getting in touch with his former colleagues, members of the underground communist party in Poland, as well as with political sympathizers and friends that he became acquainted with when he was a Soviet official in pre-war Vilnius. Step by step, a communist underground cell, with Witenberg at its head, was established in the ghetto. Witenberg's experience in clandestine underground operations in pre-war Poland was priceless in his secret ghetto political undertakings.

Resistance to the Nazi occupiers was an important component of any underground political activity in the ghetto, and an expression of the struggle for individual survival. In fact, the main objective of any form of resistance was survival. Death with dignity was the second choice. Resistance could be passive or active; individual or collective. Jewish existence was in itself an expression of resistance, and Jewish political and cultural activity in the ghetto was a statement of spiritual opposition. Under Nazi rule every Jew resisted death. By learning to cope with tribulations to which few ordinary mortals were ever exposed in our modern times he, or she, struggled against the overwhelming odds of daily existence.

Active resistance to Nazi oppression could take a variety of different forms. In most instances it was conditioned by the kind of weapon the Jew was able to procure. Individual armed resistance to Nazi occupation was in most cases an act of desperation and a sign of moral strength. It was an open challenge to the Nazi oppressive machine and an expression of defiance to a society which sanctified mass murder and ignored the value of human life. Moreover, by refusing to accept the verdict of the torturer, and at the first opportunity trying to punish the tyrant instead, the intended victim was asserting one's personal dignity. He or she was reaffirming that regardless of what the oppressor might claim his or her life, as the life of any other human being, was sacred and not subject to wanton savagery.

Individual resistance, however, was almost always doomed to failure. The most a downtrodden Jew could do was kill or wound one's oppressor with the help of a gun or knife, only to be murdered , in turn, on the spot by another Nazi. Only in rare instances could the Jew delude the vigilant eye of the Nazis and escape their pursuit which inevitably followed. But even then only those with good connections in the non-Jewish community, and a place to hide outside the ghetto or camp, had a chance to survive. But most had nowhere to go, and would eventually be hunted down by the Nazis. Thus, the relationship between armed resistance and survival was tenuous at best, and armed resistance could not guarantee survival. It turned, however, the oppressor and his victim into relative equals. It raised the victim to a new level of spiritual fortitude and repudiated a system which legalized the mass murder of innocent people. Regardless, whether the armed Jew survived or was killed by the tyrant, the gun turned him or her from a downtrodden and despised insect into a human being again.

It is necessary, however, to note that armed resistance to Nazi oppression was not only a political and military choice. It was also an ethical decision. There was often a high price to be paid for the sheer hope of survival. It was well known in the ghetto that once a resistance fighter was killed or apprehended by the Nazis, most members of his or her family would be executed by the occupiers. Hence, the hope to survive by one, could endanger the lives of many others. The Germans used the fear of collective punishment as a means of pressure to intimidate the ghetto Jews, and discourage them from joining the armed resistance movement. The decree of collective responsibility and punishment closed for many the way of escape to the forest, because every resident of the ghetto who managed to disappear unnoticed from the ghetto was, in a way, condemning his or her family and neighbours to danger and possible death. Superintendents of communal dwellings, as well as brigadiers and leaders of work gangs, were made responsible for those in their care, and were ordered to report daily about those missing. Out of fear for their own safety many ghetto residents were turned unwittingly into stool pigeons. They were forced and expected to inform to the police about those missing from the ghetto, and about anyone's intentions to escape or resist.

Individual calls for armed resistance to the oppressor were heard in Vilnius from the day the Germans entered the city, and long before organized resistance took any shape. Early in September 1941, the day the Jews of Vilnius were driven into the ghetto, Yechiel Sheinbaum, who later became the leader of the Second Fighting Organization in the ghetto, publicly called on his fellow Jews to resist to Nazi oppression.

Active manifestations of unorganized individual resistance to the Nazis were apparent already in the early days of occupation. Many Jews refused to obey Nazi orders and preferred to be killed in their homes, rather than follow to places of mass slaughter. In December 1941, during one of the deportation actions from the Vilnius ghetto, when many members of the Jewish underworld were rounded up and driven to Ponary for execution, the unarmed so-called "shtarke," or strongmen, disobeyed the orders of those escorting them and refused to move. With their bare hands the "shtarke" started a fight with their armed guards. Many Jews were killed on the spot, but some managed to escape, and later turned up back in the ghetto, the only place where they could hide for the time being.[3]

There were instances when individual Jews, infused with the desire of revenge, refused to submit to their Nazi torturers and attacked their jailors instead. The havoc among the murderers, created by such individual outbursts, made possible the escape of some other Jews who were otherwise doomed to be slaughtered on the spot. In a report about the situation in Lithuania in April 1943, submitted to Berlin in May 1943, *Obersturmfuhrer* Muller and *Obersturmfuhrer* Stutz declared that "...during the shooting one Jew attacked *Unterscharfuhrer* Willa and wounded him, stabbing him twice in the back and once in the head. He was taken to the Vilna hospital... while about fifty Jews escaped, a member of the Lithuanian auxiliary police was wounded; his condition is serious."[4]

These individual examples of Jewish personal courage and determination notwithstanding, it was clear, at that time, to every politically conscious individual in the ghetto, who sought political or resistance activity, that no single isolated group could wage successful battle against the Nazi oppressor, and that the cause of resistance to the Nazi extermination machine could be advanced only by unified action with the participation of all political groups in the ghetto. Organized armed resistance could not guarantee physical survival, and, in fact, the opposite was often the case, but the group provided its members with a sense of belonging, as well as with spiritual and emotional support. The sheer notion of resisting the enemy's vile and pernicious racist ideology and the determination not to submit to his overwhelming military force, provided members of the organized resistance with a sense of self-esteem and a realization that they served a worthwhile cause. In practical terms well organized armed resistance groups had a better possibility to procure arms, carry out acts of sabotage, and gather useful intelligence information. It was obvious that in order to produce results resistance to Nazi oppression would have to involve a communal effort rather than individual endeavour. Hence, at the early stages of ghetto life the main and perhaps the most important objective of the underground political forces in the ghetto was of an organizational rather than military or political nature.

In the early days of occupation Jewish political activists sought to reestablish their former social and political ties. Most political groups, however, were small, depleted by the loss of many young males to the so-called pre-ghetto Lithuanian "catchers," or to the early surprise Nazi extermination actions within the ghetto. These groups were loosely organized, not homogeneous, and most members lacked experience in underground activity. Besides, except for the communists, members of most other political organizations, such as various Zionist groups or the *Bund*, were just coming out from their former Soviet underground. And yet, in addition to the communists, members of various Zionist groups such as the *Hashomer Hatsair*, the Revisionists, or the Yiddishist *Bund* managed to get together, renew old contacts, and initiate political activity.

The first public call for resistance to the Nazis was expressed on 1 January 1942, at a Zionist meeting, of more than a hundred people. They gathered in the ghetto, at the house at 2 Strashun Street, to commemorate the Jews murdered in Ponary[5]. Aba Kovner, a poet and Zionist leader, read at that gathering the Proclamation, which called for rebellion and resistance to Nazi oppression. It stated:

> "They shall not take us like sheep to the slaughter! Jewish youth, do not be led astray. Of the 80,000 Jews in the 'Jerusalem of Lithuania' (Vilna) only 20,000 have remained. Before our eyes they tore from us our parents, our brothers and sisters,....
> All those who were taken away from the ghetto never came back. All the roads of the Gestapo lead to Ponary. And Ponary is death! Doubters! Cast off all illusions.... Ponary is not a camp - all are shot there.... *Let us not go as sheep to slaughter!*
> It is true that we are weak and defenceless, but resistance is the only reply to the enemy!

Brothers! It is better to fall as free fighters, then to live by the grace of the murderers.
Resist! To the last breath."[6]

Years later Kovner declared, that it

" was I who wrote the famous phrase 'like sheep to slaughter' - a phrase that haunts me now wherever I go.... It was written in December 1941 as the heading of a leaflet that called for rebellion. The aim of the leaflet was to shake ghetto inhabitants out of their conviction that they were standing   before a situation of total destruction....and that the only way out was to go to their death with honour.... The phrase that I used then must not be taken out of context.... I had never thought that the sheep had anything to be ashamed of."[7]

The first attempts to create a unified resistance organization in the ghetto were fruitless. The individual political doctrines of different underground groups in the ghetto were so distinct that no ideological compromise was possible, and that the creation of an organization with a single theoretical agenda was almost impossible. The pragmatic approach to life, however, necessitated by ghetto conditions, forced the leaders of the Jewish political underground to seek ways of rapprochement and compromise. They were compelled to accept the reality that a time had come when ideological and political differences were secondary to matters of ethnic and racial identity, and that issues of national unity were to be placed, at least for the time being, above ideological and class interests. The enemy paid little attention to the political views of different Jews. To the Nazis they were all equal. They envisaged a common destiny for all of them. They were all doomed. In view of the above it was obvious to everyone that it was preferable to fight and try to survive together rather than wage battle in small groups, and face inevitable extinction apart.

The decision to form a unified resistance organization was an important step, but leaders of different political parties continued to have difficulty in agreeing on the general strategy and tactical moves of this proposed new fighting body. Some believed that it was the duty of Jewish resistance fighters to defend the helpless   ghetto population and put up a fight within the walls of the ghetto, when the liquidation of the ghetto and the deportation of its residents would be certain. Others recognized the futility of combat inside the ghetto, and believed that a greater number of Jews could be saved by leaving the ghetto as soon as possible in order to join the pro-Soviet partisans in the nearby forests.

It might appear to the uninitiated observer that the Zionists, to whom Nazi fascism and Soviet communism were equally abhorrent, were to follow the first option, while the communist who followed Marxist ideology and Soviet political judgement would prefer the second one. In Vilnius that was not the case, and there were many varieties from this general pattern. Despite the fact that Aba Kovner, the Zionist leader, claimed that "uprising and armed defence were the only honourable resorts for the Jews," [8] many Zionists wanted to leave the ghetto and join the partisans in the forest as soon as possible, while some communists advocated the opposite. Paradoxically Witenberg was one of them. He "was mostly responsible for persuading his fellow leaders that the aim of the F.P.O. must be armed resistance inside the ghetto and that leaving for the forest to become partisans would be tantamount to desertion and cowardice." [9]

Formally, 21 January 1942 is regarded as the day that denotes the beginning of organized Jewish armed resistance to Nazi occupation in the Vilnius ghetto. On that day representatives of a number of different political groups gathered at 6 Rudnicka Street, in the room of Joseph Glazman, the leader of the Zionists-Revisionists, to assert their resolve not to submit any longer to Nazi tyranny and to prepare for battle with the oppressor. Among the participant of that fateful meeting were the communists Yitzhak Witenberg and Chiena Borowska, Aba Kovner (*Hashomer Hatsair*), Joseph Glazman (Zionist-Revisionist), Nisan Reznik (*Hanoar Hatsioni*), and Isidore Frucht a former officer in the Polish Army. Members of the leftist *Bund* refused to participate in the meeting, because they were not ready to join an organization in which the right-wing Revisionists were also members.

The gathering adopted a resolution which proclaimed the establishment of the so-called Freedom Fighters Group, and outlined its basic tenets and mode of operation. Somewhat later the organization changed its name to F.P.O. The resolution stated, among others, that the aim of this new underground armed combat organization was to operate in the Vilnius ghetto with the purpose of unifying all forces able and willing to assist in the resistance to the Nazi occupiers. The main objective of the F.P.O. was to prepare people in the ghetto for mass armed resistance, in case the Nazis intended to liquidate the ghetto. The organization asserted its readiness to carry out acts of sabotage in Nazi occupied territory and it declared its support for the Red Army in its struggle against the Nazi invader. The F.P.O. asserted also its support to pro-Soviet partisans, fighting against Nazi occupation, and expressed readiness to join their ranks when conditions would warrant it. Y. Witenberg (pseudonym Leon) was elected commander-in-chief of the F.P.O., and A. Kovner (pseudonym Uri) and J. Glazman (pseudonym Abram) were appointed to its command staff.[10] Initially, Glazman was in charge of military affairs, and Kovner was the secretary of the organization.

In the spring of 1942, after protracted negotiations, representatives of the *Bund* agreed to join the F.P.O., and A. Khvoinik, one of their members, was coopted to the command of the organization. Similarly, N. Reznik, one of the original founding members of the F.P.O., joined the command staff. The F.P.O. command staff conducted its clandestine meetings in a variety of places, but most often at the public kitchen and the premises of the *kibbutz* at 31 Vokieciu (Niemiecka) Street, or at the home of Aba Kovner.

Under the leadership of Witenberg the F.P.O. grew steadily and, by the summer of 1943, its active membership was close to three hundred. It was composed of two battalions, each consisting of up to eight platoons. Small groups of up to five people in each formed a platoon. A. Kovner and J. Glazman were battalion commanders. Each battalion had attached a group of fighters with automatic weapons and a group of grenade throwers and miners. In addition there was a special platoon of instructors, individuals with former military training, who were teaching the fighters how to use their weapons. There was also a squad the members of which were mainly involved in military diversion and sabotage, and an intelligence unit the objective of which was, among others, to search for German military secrets, uncover Nazi secret orders, unmask Gestapo agents, and control the activity of F.P.O. members.

In the short term, the most important objective of the organization was to procure arms, and with that purpose an elaborate system of

smuggling weapons into the ghetto was developed. The F.P.O. established contacts with friendly gentiles in the city, and the first hand grenades brought into the ghetto by Aba Kovner, in January 1942, were
given to him by the Mother Superior of the Benedictine Convent in
Vilnius. Some members of the F.P.O. were employed at a large German factory which produced arms and ammunition, and was located at
Borbishok, at the outskirts of the city. Risking their lives daily they were
stealing weapons and ammunition and smuggling it into the ghetto.
Moreover, they were involved in an elaborate scheme of sabotage which
brought about much damage to the Nazi war effort. The Jews working
at Borbishok damaged the locking mechanism and put out of order 365
guns that were sent to the front. In the summer of 1942, tanks that
were ready to be sent to the Smolensk front were fitted, by Jewish workers at Borbishok, with tiny incendiary mechanisms in the petrol tanks,
and as soon as the train with the armoured vehicles was on its way a fire
broke out and the tanks went up in flames. Baruch Goldstein, an F.P.O.
fighter, took out vital parts from, and destroyed, 345 Zenith anti-
aircraft gun mechanisms and 90 machine guns that were to be sent to
the front.[11] The F.P.O. conducted also anti-Nazi sabotage activity in the
city. At one instance, in July 1942, F.P.O. fighters successfully mined a
German army munitions train.[12]

The workshops inside the ghetto were clandestinely used for the
purpose of repairing weapons and the production of explosive sub-
stances. The production of Molotov cocktails and hand grenades was
initiated within the ghetto as well. It is necessary, however, to note that
there was a serious problem with storing weapons in the ghetto. In the
congested conditions of ghetto life it was difficult to hide anything. The
more so since ghetto police informers were snooping all over and Jewish
policemen, fearful for the safety of the ghetto, were arresting those who
were suspected of having arms. Initially, the F.P.O. Was storing its weapons in secure hiding places in the cellars of 2 Strashun Street, and 14
Rudninku (Rudnicka) Street.

The F.P.O. launched a secret military combat training programme
for its members, and established contacts with Jews in other ghettos.
F.P.O. representatives informed residents of those ghettos of the danger of further Nazi atrocities and warned them of imminent Nazi killing actions. The F.P.O. organized also the operation of a clandestine

printing press, and set up a secret radio installation. Based on the radio information received, the F.P.O. issued every day a statement about the political conditions in the country and the military situation at the front. The F.P.O. provided assistance to Soviet war prisoners and the wives of Red Army commanders who were incarcerated at special premises on Subotch Street in Vilnius, supplying them with food and useful information. It also conducted a campaign in the ghetto to raise funds for the purpose of buying arms. Weapons were usually acquired from two main sources: they were bought from the local civilian population or stolen from the Germans and their Lithuanian collaborators. In both instances the attempt to procure arms was always fraught with dangerous consequences. When a Jew was caught stealing weapons or ammunition he or she was usually arrested and executed without delay.

It was always dangerous for a Jew to absent oneself from his place of work in the city and venture for whatever reason outside. Even the attempt to procure food was dangerous. A notice posted in the ghetto on 30 April 1942 stated that several Jews from the ghetto, who left their work place and went to buy food in the countryside, were shot without enquiry. There were attempts and a remote possibility of getting arms from Polish and Lithuanian anti-Nazi underground organizations in the city, but by and large these endeavours were futile.

One of the important tasks of the underground resistance movement in the ghetto was to establish contacts with, and receive practical support from, the friendly anti-Nazi underground forces outside the ghetto. There were several distinct anti-Nazi entities operating in the occupied territories. First, there were different armed partisan detachment based in the Lithuanian and Belorussian forests. Some were supporting the Red Army and the Soviet regime, others, like the Polish A.K. (*Armia Krajowa*), or Home Army, supported the Polish government in exile, in London, England, and were anti-Soviet. According to some Polish sources the A.K. had, at that time, in the Vilnius region close to 5,000 well armed and equipped members.[13]

The F.P.O. did manage to establish contacts with the A.K. in Vilnius and asked for help in the acquisition of arms. The A.K. refused to provide arms for the F.P.O., because they claimed that it was pro-Soviet, and controlled by communists.[14] Moreover, the A.K. refused even to assist the Polish communist underground in the city which was poorly armed and with limited financial resources. It is suggested, however, that individual members of the A.K. in the city provided the ghetto with practical and emotional help. Thus, Dr. Jan Kloniecki, an A.K. member, was the head of the sanitary-epidemiological department of the city health administration. He was in charge of the sanitary conditions in the ghetto, and the interment of the dead at the Jewish cemetery. Dr. Kloniecki helped smuggle medication, disinfectants, and soap into the ghetto, and he provided for the treatment in the city of Jewish children with infectious diseases.[15]

There were also independent Lithuanian groups that opposed both the Germans and the Soviets. Similarly, there were some clandestine, mainly communist underground groups, in major urban centres, which were conducting political propaganda amidst the local population. Some members of these groups were involved in sabotage, reconnaissance, intelligence, and counter-intelligence activity. The F.P.O. established contacts with both, the pro-Soviet partisans in the Lithuanian and Belorussian forests, as well as the communist underground in the city. In both instances Witenberg was the pointsman.

In the fall of 1941, a Pole Jan Przewalski, a veteran of the pre-war communist movement in Wilno, began to gather around him a small group of Polish and Belorussian communists. Early in 1942, Przewalski and the Belorussian Makar Korablikov joined the underground Union of Active Struggle (*Zwiazek Walki Czynnej*), which consisted mostly of Poles, and they soon established contacts with the ghetto underground. The Polish A.K. which was staunchly anti-communist and anti-Soviet, opposed the Union of Active Struggle and denounced some of its members to the Nazis.

At the same time a six-men group of Soviet parachutists, commanded by Albertas Kunigenas (pseudonym Alksnis), landed not far from the Jewish labour camp in Biala Waka (Baltoji Voke) where Jewish men and women, mostly from Vilnius, were employed on peat digging. The parachutists got in touch with the Jewish workers, and soon Witenberg was on his way to Biala Waka to meet the newcomers. According to some sources the meeting took place in February 1942, others suggested that it was in April 1942.[16] Still others asserted that it was in the second half of 1942.[17]

At this momentous encounter, near Biala Waka, Witenberg met

one of the parachutists, the Pole Witold Sienkiewicz (pseudonym Margis), who later became the political commissar of a major pro-Soviet partisan detachment, not far from Vilnius in the Rudninku forest (Puszcza Rudnicka). After the war Sienkiewicz was a highly placed party and security official in post-war Poland. Sienkiewicz officially recognized the F.P.O. as a part of the Lithuanian partisan movement and appointed Witenberg, B. Shereshnievski, and Borowska to the Vilnius city communist party committee, with the rights to coopt new members. Shereshnievski was assigned the job of first secretary of the city communist party organization.

In March 1943 Juozas Vitas (pseudonym for Jonas Valunas) arrived in Vilnius. Vitas, born in 1899, was a communist party member since 1919. In his youth he fought for the establishment of Soviet power in Lithuania. Between the wars he lived and worked most of the time in the USSR. [18] When in 1940 Vilnius became the capital Soviet Lithuania, Vitas returned to Vilnius and became the mayor of the city. Soon after his arrival to Vilnius, in the spring of 1943, Vitas became involved in anti-Nazi underground work. At first, he formed a Lithuanian anti-Nazi organization, and later attempted to unify and coordinate the activity of all clandestine communist and progressive anti-Nazi forces. On 5 May 1943 the Polish, Lithuanian, and Jewish anti-Nazi leftist underground organizations in Vilnius came together to form the Vilnius communist anti-fascist committee. Vitas was elected chairman, and Przewalski his deputy. The other members of the committee were Korablikov, Witenberg, Shereshnievski, and Waclaw Kozlowski. [19]

Witenberg's active political involvement with the non-Jewish communist underground in the city exposed him, together with his communist comrades, to the danger of being denounced to the Gestapo, or the Lithuanian security police, by the numerous spies, Nazi agents, or just anti-communists residents of Vilnius. In the ghetto it was much easier to remain inconspicuous and hide in the Jewish mass. Moreover, there was little likelihood of a Jew being denounced by a fellow Jew to the Nazis.

The dangers of Jewish participation in the communist underground activity in the city notwithstanding, the F.P.O. leadership approved of Witenberg's participation in the work of the Vilnius communist antifascist underground, and valued highly his personal contribution to the resistance movement in the ghetto. According to his comrades-in-arms Witenberg was a man of practical wisdom, rock-like courage, and un-failing self-control. Thirteen years of underground activity in the Polish Communist Party heightened his self-assurance. His face reflected cour-age and self-confidence, and he exercised in the F.P.O. almost dictatorial influence.[20]

B. Shereshnievski, an active underground communist and F.P.O. member, declared that Witenberg "was a politically educated man. In the most difficult situations of our struggle in the ghetto he would find a way out. He was courageous and wise. He would approach each situa-tion coolly and in his characteristically relaxed manner." [21] A. Kovner, the man who took over the leadership of the F.P.O. after Witenberg's surrender to the Nazis, asserted that Witenberg "was one of the most righteous people he ever encountered in life. He was mostly affected by Witenberg's simple and objective approach to problems." [22]

Witenberg's pre-war underground communist activity, his party service in the Soviet days, and his personal acquaintance with the lead-ers of the anti-Nazi communist movement in occupied Lithuania, had positive as well as negative repercussions. Witenberg was trusted by his communist comrades in the city and was accepted by them as one of their own, yet their immediate aims differed considerably from the ob-jectives of the ghetto underground. As most communist activists Witenberg was influenced by communist ideology and propaganda and he overestimated the ability and desire of the communist underground in Lithuania to provide practical help to the resistance fighters in the ghetto. Indeed, the city communist underground provided moral sup-port to the ghetto fighters, and it shared its political and intelligence information with the ghetto resistance movement, but it was small and weak and it could do little to assist the ghetto fighters in the case of open struggle and military confrontation with the occupiers. The ghetto underground, in turn, provided the city communist underground with money, arms, and the use of a clandestine printing press.

The dedication of Witenberg to the anti-Nazi cause, his personal human qualities, and his capability to lead were beyond question. But his one-sided political education acquired in his underground communist cell in pre-war Poland, and in the days of Soviet rule in Western Belorussia and Lithuania, often deprived him of the ability to evaluate political and military situations objectively and view life and history from a wider, non-partisan, perspective. Thus, at a gathering of close underground associates in the ghetto at which the day of international labour solidarity, 1 May 1943, was celebrated, and the Warsaw ghetto uprising, which started on 20 April 1943, was commemorated, Witenberg delivered a lengthy speech. He made a general overview of the situation at the eastern front, placing special emphasis on the success of the Soviet army, and he provided his listeners with an overly optimistic appraisal of the existing state of affairs. He "expressed the opinion that when the front and the Red Army will be getting closer we will have to move into the city, and raise the whole population to help liberate the city." [23]

At another instance, when the question of joining the partisans in the forest was discussed, Witenberg stated bluntly that "when we will find out that the Nazis intend to destroy the ghetto we will call upon the ghetto population to break through the gates of the ghetto and under the cover of our arms move into the forest."[24] According to Witenberg's plan the F.P.O. fighters, supported by the ghetto Jews, would set on fire German military installations before leaving the city for the forest.[25] It was most unfortunate that Witenberg the visionary was unable to assess the situation objectively, and that he planned to accomplish the impossible. His appraisal of the situation at the front was unsubstantiated, and his reliance on the support of the local population was at best naive.

Witenberg's commitment to, and faith in, the communist underground in the city affected his resistance philosophy in the ghetto and it reinforced his determination to fight the Nazis within the ghetto. At the same time, it deterred members of the ghetto underground resistance movement from escaping to the forest. In the spring of 1943 Colonel F. Markov, a former teacher in Western Belorussia, and presently the commander of the Soviet partisan brigade named after Marshal K. Voroshilov, became aware of the existence of an armed resistance movement in the ghetto. He approached then the F.P.O. command and in a letter exhorted Jewish youths to leave the ghetto and join his unit.[26] Markov's stipulation, however, that only armed men could join his brigade was unacceptable to the F.P.O. leadership. Moreover, its reliance on the city communist underground, and resoluteness to wage battle inside the ghetto, precluded the early departure of any F.P.O. members to the forest.

Witenberg was a loyal communist and his faith in the communist ideology was unshakable. In his mind, the communists, armed with the allegedly most advanced revolutionary philosophy of Marxism-Leninism, were infallible. Witenberg was unaware yet, at that time, of Stalin's anti-Semitism and the purges of his former colleagues and political associates, and he believed that only the victory of Marxist-Leninist revolution could save East European Jewry. No wonder, in certain instances Witenberg placed his commitment to the party above his allegiance to the ghetto underground resistance movement. Thus, for example, occasionally he kept from his F.P.O colleagues information obtained in the city, but essential for the safety of the ghetto and its underground resistance movement, depriving thus his ghetto colleagues of the possibility to make proper decisions in most dangerous times. In due time it became known that Witenberg "hid from the underground the fact that a week earlier the communist central committee, of which Witenberg was a member, had been arrested in the city."[27] Moreover, he concealed from te F.P.O. command that in addition to being a member of the communist resistance underground, he was also a member of the underground city communist party committee. The situation was indeed paradoxical. While the F.P.O. considered Witenberg as its representative in the communist resistance underground in the city, the communist party in the city regarded him as its representative to, and watchman of, the F.P.O.

In the spring of 1943 the communist underground in the city suffered an irreparable blow, from which it was almost impossible to recover. The Lithuanian Juozas Vaitkevicius, a Gestapo secret agent, managed to penetrate the communist cell in the city, and denounce to the German secret police most of its active membership. On 19 June 1943 the Gestapo arrested Vitas. His arrest had far reaching consequences for Witenberg, for the ghetto resistance movement, and for the ghetto in general. On 9 July 1943 the Germans arrested W. Kozlowski, another member of the city underground communist party committee, together with his mother, wife and children. They were all submitted to ruthless interrogation, the ususal Gestapo torture, and were eventually all murdered. Kozlowski was the contact man between the ghetto communists leaders, Witenberg and Shereshnievski, and the city party organization. Occasionally he would even come to party meetings conducted within the ghetto. It was most likely that Kozlowski, tortured by the Nazis mercilessly, broke down and named Witenberg as one of the members of the city communist party committee.[28] Initially, some members of the F.P.O. command suspected that Kozlowski was a provocateur and a Gestapo agent, but they later realized that was not the case.

After the arrest and the interrogation of Vitas and Kozlowski Bruno Kittel, the German security officer in charge of Jewish affairs in Vilnius, arrived in the ghetto and demanded that the Jewish ghetto authorities arrest Witenberg and hand him over to the Gestapo for interrogation. Kittel threatened that in the event his request was not complied with the Germans would proceed with the immediate liquidation of the Vilnius ghetto. Kittel tried, however, to reassure the Jewish ghetto administration, and promised that as soon as the interrogation will be completed Witenberg will be brought back in to the ghetto. In order to convince the Jews in the ghetto of their good intentions the Germans used a cunning trick. They arrested a Jewish police officer in the ghetto and after having interrogated him set him free the next day. Being well familiar with the treacherous nature of Nazi politics, Witenberg did not trust the German promises, and as soon as he found out about the menace to his safety he went into hiding. The Jewish police tried hard to find him, but failed to apprehend him.

On 15 July 1943, Gens invited members of the F.P.O. command to his office for an ostensible information session. Witenberg and his colleagues honoured this invitation and came to meet Gens. According to N. Reznik, Witenberg, Borowska, Kovner, Krizhovski, and Reznik participated in the meeting. At the time of the meeting several Lithuanian policemen appeared on the scene and asked for Witenberg. Kovner replied that no such individual was present in the room. Gens then allegedly pointed at Witenberg and the Lithuanian policemen arrested him.[29] According to Ruzka Korchak, one of the F.P.O. insiders, Witenberg was then handed over to several Gestapo men and Lithuanian policemen who accompanied him to the gates of the ghetto. They did not reach, however, their intended destination. The F.P.O. did not relent and decided to fight for its leader. It happened all suddenly. On his way to the ghetto gate Witenberg heard loud calls from his F.P.O. colleagues to the effect that "Witenberg is arrested, everyone to the gate in order to set him free," This was when Witenberg eluded the vigilant eyes of his jailors and disappeared in the darkness of the night. The Germans did not yield, and gave chase in an attempt to recapture him, but to no avail.[30] In no time was Witenberg whisked away by his comrades to a new hiding place. The German authorities, however, did not abandon their original intentions. "At dawn on 16 July the ghetto was faced with an ultimatum. Witenberg had to surrender before 6 P.M., or aircraft summoned from Kaunas would set the ghetto on fire and destroy it together with its inhabitants." [31]

16 July 1943 was a day of extreme tension in the ghetto. By stressing continuously that only the surrender of Witenberg could save the remaining Jews of Vilnius, the Jewish ghetto authorities manipulated the public mood in the ghetto and orchestrated a confrontation between the general ghetto population and the underground resistance movement. Panic struck the ghetto. Crowds of people gathered on the streets in search of information. Ghetto residents accepted in good faith the clamour that the ghetto was imperiled just because one man, a communist into the bargain, refused to surrender. Gens and Desler mobilized several hundred toughs and ruffians, members of the Jewish underworld, who armed with sticks and bludgeons roamed the ghetto streets in search of Witenberg.

It was impossible to know, at that time, whether the German threat to bomb the ghetto was real or just a bluff; whether it was a serious intention of collective punishment or just a means to intimidate the ghetto population. However, since the brutality and ruthlessness of the Nazis was well known, no one wanted to challenge them and put their real intention to a test.   In the meantime Witenberg was hiding, and moving from place to place. At first he was hiding in the room of Zinka Barkan (later Malecki), but after a while even his comrades in the F.P.O command did not know exactly about his whereabouts.[32] According to Zhenia Malecki, who claims to have been a neighbour of the Witenberg family in the ghetto, on 16 July 1943 Witenberg's wife, Etel, a little slim woman, stayed behind in her room with her younger son.[33] Witenberg's older, sixteen year old, son was allegedly already involved in resistance activity conducted by the F.P.O.

The F.P.O. was faced with a dilemma. There was a real possibility that in order to protect its leader, instead of fighting the Nazis it would have to confront the exasperated ghetto Jews. The F.P.O. was under tremendous pressure, and its command had difficulty in arriving at a final decision of how to act. The determination of Witenberg's fate, however, was left to Witenberg himself and to the narrow circle of his political friends, members of the communist party organization in the ghetto. When the communist leadership in the ghetto realized that Kozlowski betrayed only Witenberg; that he failed to disclose to the Nazis that an underground resistance organization existed in the ghetto, or to provide the Gestapo with the names of the other communists in the ghetto, it caved in and Witenberg's closest friends decided that he must surrender in order to save the ghetto if not from total destruction then at least from internal civil strife.

Eventually the leaders of the communist cell in the ghetto informed the F.P.O. command about their decision, and the F.P.O leaders agreed with the proposed solution. A delegation composed of the communists Sonia Madesker and Borowska, and the F.P.O. representative N. Reznik, managed then to establish contact with Witenberg and pass on to him their decision. Initially Witenberg refused to accept the decision of his party comrades. He was not prepared to give himself up and he disappeared again, trying even to escape disguised as a woman. He claimed, that if necessary, he was ready to fight the Nazis, disregarding the fact that this would endanger the existence of the ghetto itself. He firmly believed that the ghetto was doomed anyway, and that his surrender would not save the ghetto anyway. In the end Witenberg gave in, and was ready to accept the decision of his colleagues. He met then, in his hiding place, with the members of the F.P.O. command staff. At this last meeting with Witenberg were present Kovner, Glazman, Khvoinik, Borowska, and Reznik At this point, Witenberg asserted that he was prepared to commit suicide, rather then fall into the hands of the dreaded Gestapo. His colleagues managed, however, to persuade him that there was still a chance to return alive from the Gestapo, and that in any case he will be provided with poison for any eventuality.[34]

According to Aba Kovner Witenberg's decision to surrender was his own. Kovner stressed that had Witenberg ordered the F.P.O. to fight, it would follow the orders of its commander.[35] Witenberg was hiding, at that time, in the room of his lover Edzia Freedman. When Witenberg handed over his gun to Aba Kovner, and appointed him commander-in-chief of the F.P.O., Ms. Freedman became hysterical and started to scream, accusing those present of treachery and murder, and of sacrificing Witenberg in vain. She held on to Witenberg and would not let him go. In the end he set himself free from her embraces with force, and went to see Gens before his final surrender.[36]

It appears that Witenberg's lover did survive the war and returned to Vilnius. When in 1946 Jokubas Josade, a Lithuanian Jewish playwright and literary critic, intended to write a play about Witenberg he approached the woman in question. It turned out that she was the daughter of a wealthy Jew from the Polish city Lodz who arrived in Vilnius as a refugee just before the war. She was still young, attractive, and smart.[37] Soon the woman disappeared from sight having apparently been repatriated to Poland.

The whole ordeal exposed Witenberg to extreme psychological pressure and the weight of moral responsibility. His colleagues and closest friends tried to impress upon him that the fate of the ghetto was in his hands, and that only his surrender could save the remnants of the Jewish community in Vilnius. Paradoxically it could appear, that ominous day of 16 July 1943, that not the Nazi murderers, but rather Witenberg was responsible for the danger to, and imminent death of, the ghetto residents. Faced with mounting pressure, of friends and foes alike, Witenberg resisted no longer and decided to abide by the decision of his party colleagues. By accepting a decision with which he did not agree Witenberg exhibited party loyalty and discipline, as well as strength of character, courage, and determination.

Prior to giving himself up, Witenberg warned his colleagues that if they surrender him to the Nazis their own destruction would follow soon, and the ghetto would be liquidated without offering any resistance.[38] He said that "it has never happened that an organization would surrender its leader. Any party which acts this way is bankrupt." The F.P.O. and the ghetto communist leadership, however, realized that all their resistance plans, based on common action with the communist underground in the city, had been shattered and they capitulated.

It appeared thus that Witenberg was betrayed twice. The first time, by his communist political associates in the city who could not withstand Nazi torture. The second time he was abandoned by his Jewish resistance colleagues [39] who were led to believe that by surrendering

Witenberg they will save, or at least postpone the destruction, of the ghetto, and buy time for themselves. "On the day Witenberg was arrested Gens told [the F.P.O. leaders] that [the arrest] was not connected with the ghetto underground, but because of his [Witenberg's] ties with the communist underground in the city. That was when his comrades decided that he must give himself up."[40]

The ghetto Jewish leaders, including both Gens and the F.P.O. command failed, however, to realize, at that time, that the F.P.O. challenge to Gens and the Jewish police, when Witenberg was arrested for the first time, on 15 July 1943, and later set free by his colleagues, sealed in a sense the fate of the ghetto. By freeing Witenberg from arrest, the F.P.O. illustrated to the Germans that the underground was stronger than the ghetto administration and the Jewish police, and that Gens could no longer be relied upon to control the situation in the ghetto.

The evening of that ominous day of 16 July 1943 Witenberg marched to the ghetto gates, where a Gestapo car waited for him, as a proud and courageous man. But the sight of his downfall was tragic. Everyone in the ghetto knew that they saw Witenberg for the last time; that there would be no return for him from the German clutches. Paradoxically, most ghetto residents felt relief. They were made to believe that the presence of Witenberg in the ghetto was tantamount to danger, and once he was gone the hazard would pass and life in the ghetto would continue as before. That was, of course, another illusion. At the Gestapo headquarters Witenberg's case was handed over to Max Gross, the special German interrogator for partisan affairs. The next morning Witenberg was found dead in one of the corridors of the Gestapo headquarters. According to some sources "Witenberg was tortured to death,"[41] "his hair were burned, his eyes pierced, and his broken arms tied behind his back." [42]

According to evidence uncovered in the Lithuanian Security, formerly KGB, Archives, a certain Ginzburg, who in the summer of 1943 worked as a stoker in the Vilnius Gestapo, informed the Jewish underground in the ghetto that Witenberg was murdered in prison and his body was cut into pieces with the help of a saw. The same information was allegedly brought into the ghetto by Mr. Kamermacher who was, at that time, the leader of the gang of Jewish workers employed at the local Gestapo facilities.[43] According to other, more reliable, sources Witenberg committed suicide, before the Nazis could interrogate and torture him, with the help of a dose of cyanide of potassium, given to him by Gens.[44] According to N. Reznik, S. Desler provided Witenberg with a poison pill of delayed action which Witenberg swallowed before his departure from the ghetto. The poison became active, and killed Witenberg, seven hours later, when he was already in the Gestapo jail.[45] Witenberg's determination to commit suicide was a desperate, yet courageous, deed. It spared him of any unforseen consequences of interrogation and Nazi torture, and from dying a slow and humiliating death.[46]

The tragic departure of Witenberg was a tremendous personal sacrifice and also a mark of defeat for the F.P.O. This sacrifice was allegedly supposed to save the Vilnius ghetto from immediate destruction. In reality, however, it did little to prevent the realization of the Nazi "Final Solution" in Vilnius. And yet, the two months between the Witenberg debacle and the final liquidation of the ghetto made it possible for hundreds of Jews to escape from the ghetto and avoid immediate destruction. Some managed to join the pro-Soviet partisans in the adjoining forests, while others escaped to the city, into well prepared in advance hiding places.

Aba Kovner, the new leader of the F.P.O, understood well the arduousness of the task with which he was entrusted. He was also aware of the fact that henceforth the responsibility for the surrender of Witenberg will weigh heavily on the conscience of the members of the F.P.O. command. Moreover, he understood that in the future this experience might hamper the effectiveness of F.P.O. operations. "History will probably blame us for this," stated the protocol of the F.P.O. staff meeting, headed by Kovner. "It is probable that no one will ever entirely understand the situation in which we were placed and the actions which resulted from our great responsibility to the ghetto and to the masses against whom we could not, indeed might not fight."[47]

Aba Kovner, a twenty-five year old poet and politician, was a committed ideological Zionist visionary, but he was not an individual with military training or practical combat experience. According to his wife, Vitka Kempner, he was indecisive, and always saw two sides to the same issue. Moreover, he always doubted decisions once accepted and approved.[48] These traits of Kovner's character affected the decision-making process of the F.P.O. and its ability to act in a decisive and resolute manner. On the surface, influenced by both, Witenberg and the uprising in the Warsaw ghetto, Kovner continued to stick to the original plan of fighting the Nazis within the walls of the ghetto, while at the same time broaching the idea of escaping to the forest.

The Witenberg affair unsettled the relative tranquillity in the ghetto. It placed the relationship of the F.P.O. with the ghetto population in a new perspective, and it heightened the tension between the Jewish underground and the Jewish administration of the ghetto. It accelerated also contacts with the partisans and provided those who intended to join the partisans in the forest with a new sense of urgency. Indeed, after the surrender of Witenberg , Joseph Glazman called for the immediate departure to the forest. Some members of the F.P.O. leadership, including J. Kaplan and N. Reznik, supported Glazman, but others, including its new leader Kovner and Khvoinik, were still against it.

Soon, however, the F.P.O. command became seriously concerned for the safety of its leaders, and it was induced to sanction the departure of a group of its members to the forest. On 24 July 1943, Joseph Glazman, with a group of F.P.O. fighters, left the ghetto and moved through Nowa Wilejka in the direction of the Narocz partisan region in Western Belorussia. In Nowa Wilejka the group was joined by some youngsters from the adjoining pit-digging camp. On its way, however, the group was confronted by a German ambush, and some of its members were killed in battle. With the help of the so-called dog-tags, or metal identity discs, which every Jew was supposed to wear at all times, the Germans were able to identify some of those killed. A day later Gestapo agents arrived in the ghetto and demanded that all family members of those who had gone to the forest, as well as the brigadiers of the work gangs that the partisans belonged to, be arrested and turned over to the German security police. In all some eighty Jews were removed from the ghetto and taken to Ponary for execution. In addition, in reprisal for the escape of some workers from the pit-digging camp in Nowa Wilejka, and their attempt to join the Soviet partisans, the camps in Nowa Wilejka and Bezdany were completely destroyed, and all Jews employed there were murdered. Glazman, and the remaining fighters who escaped the German ambush, did manage to reach the Narocz forests and join there the Jewish partisan detachment. Unfortunately, somewhat later, Glazman was killed in battle with the overwhelming Nazi forces.

In the year and a half of the F.P.O. existence members of its command staff managed to establish close personal friendship ties, with each other, across party lines. In the summer of 1943, however, despite the increasing complications in the relationship between the F.P.O., Gens, and the German authorities, cracks in the until recently unified multi-party structure of the F.P.O. also became apparent. The *Bund,* for example, disagreed with some F.P.O. decisions and refused to support some policies adopted by the F.P.O. command. The F.P.O. command staff, for example, resolved that even if only one of its leaders will be apprehended by the ghetto Jewish police it will fight, if necessary with arms in hand, to protect its members from the Jewish police. The *Bund* declared that it was prepared to support the F.P.O. only as long as its main objective was to defend the ghetto Jews, but that any military confrontation between different groups of Jews inside the ghetto was a provocation and would not be tolerated.[49] Not all board members of the *Bund* approved, however, of such approach, and the *Bund,* representatives in the F.P.O. command refused to support the adopted decision by the board of *Bund.*[50]

The outcome of the Witenberg affair had a damaging effect on the image and credibility of the F.P.O., and it paralysed, to a degree, the effectiveness of its actions. Unnerved by the departure of its leader, and weakened by internal political squabbles, the F.P.O. failed to assess realistically the new situation and continued to operate on political and military premises adopted at a time when the conditions in the ghetto were vastly different.

After the arrest of Witenberg, and in particular after the departure of Joseph Glazman with the F.P.O. fighters to the forest, the polarization between different interest groups in the ghetto was becoming more apparent and continuously growing . On the one hand, there were in the ghetto several major underground resistance groups, well organized, disciplined, and with a set plan of action. On the other, there were many individuals in the ghetto, some unaware even of the existence of the F.P.O., yet determined not to surrender without a fight. There were also many small, politically unaffiliated groups of youngsters, the main objective of which was to obtain arms, seek contacts with guides from the forest, and leave the ghetto as soon as possible. At first, the F.P.O. tried to control the underground situation in the ghetto and discouraged any independent resistance activity. In the summer of 1943, however, when the situation in the ghetto became extremely volatile and clandestine resistance activity in the ghetto was no longer secret to any one, it became impossible to control the actions of individual Jews who were bent on trying anything that could increase their chances for survival.

At the same time there were many Jews in the ghetto, in particular intellectuals, who had little faith in the feasibility of armed resistance to the Nazis in the ghetto, and who were convinced that if the Germans will not be provoked the destruction of the ghetto was not imminent. Hence, they perceived Jewish underground resistance fighters not as heroes, bent on opposing the murderous Nazi designs, but rather as extremists who were endangering the very existence of the ghetto. Moreover, since they believed that the proliferation of arms in the ghetto endangered its existence, these individuals, including the well known scholar philologists, Zelik Kalmanovitsh, urged the Jewish ghetto administration and the ghetto police to introduce stringent controls in order to stop Jews from bringing in arms into the ghetto. In July 1943 Kalmanovitsh wrote in his diary that

> "It cannot be that our extremists believe in the possibility of victory....Then why make a useless uprising? The strength of the prisoner lies only in his continued existence.... In reality, when these people speak of the so-called "honour" which they defend they bring disgrace upon the tens of thousands that perished. These martyrs are in truth no less worthy than those who took to the sword... Only cowards and confused people can think of bringing in arms here." [51]

Kalmanovitsh was obviously expressing the view of the members of the Jewish ghetto administration, as well as of those Jews who believed the German promises, and continued to delude themselves that the ghetto will survive for the foreseeable future. A note posted, on 1 August 1943, in the *Geto Yedies* (Ghetto News), entitled "Sorrow and Anger," was in a similar vein. It stated that "the responsibility is upon those who have separated themselves from the ghetto community and abandoned all of its serious tasks, knowing quite well that in this way they are putting in danger the existence of the whole ghetto and first of all the lives of their dear ones. They are responsible for spilt blood."[52]

The plan of action of the F.P.O. in these difficult times was guided by policy documents adopted early in the spring of 1943. Thus, on 4 April 1943, the F.P.O. promulgated and circulated among its members the newly adopted so-called Battle Orders of the F.P.O. The objective of a Supplement to the Standing Orders , issued by the F.P.O. Commander soon after, was to provide answers to several rhetorical questions, and clarify the F.P.O. position. "How will the F.P.O. react in the event of a partial destruction of the ghetto?" was the first question posed. The answers that followed were supposed to elucidate the intended F.P.O. course of action in the envisaged circumstance. They stated:

"1. The F.P.O. will move out into battle when the existence of the ghetto as a whole is threatened.
2. It may be that there will be various kinds of murder - *Aktionen* of a local character or reprisals by the Gestapo for 'crimes,' that may cost the lives of individuals, or of tens or hundreds of Jews.
3. It is our view that the life of every single Jew is worthy of defence and must not be abandoned to the murderers without resistance.
4. The F.P.O., however, is not a large military force which can enter into a battle of equals with the enemy, and it can not and will not come out in defence of each, single Jewish life.
5. The F.P.O., which is the spearhead of the remainder of the Jewish Community (not only in Vilna) could, by premature action bring about its own premature destruction, leaving the ghetto without any defence at all, without the F.P.O., the only organization capable of fighting.
6. This kind of action would be quixotic, a suicidal tactic. Furthermore, Jews might condemn us as provocateurs, and this might cause us to fight against our own brethren.
7. But just as premature action would be irresponsible so action delayed too long would be criminal.
8. The F.P.O. will move out in such an *Aktion* when it is estimated that the beginning of the end has come; at that point it will no longer be a question of the numbers involved in the *Aktion*.
9. The Command Staff will decide when the time has come to move into battle. It will judge the situation on the basis of sources of information which are available and open to it.

THE THREE TRAGIC HEROES OF THE VILNIUS GHETTO

10. Our inadequate supply of arms justifies the fact that the F.P.O. cannot go into action at all times. But our inadequate arms cannot justify under any circumstances the avoiding of fighting when the whole existence of the ghetto is threatened.

When total destruction threatens us we must come out to fight whatever the position regarding weapons; we must come out even if we have no arms and must fight with our bare hands."

Another question, in the F.P.O. Commander's Supplement to the Standing Orders inquired brusquely: "Should we not go to the forest immediately?" The answers that followed clarified the issue:

"1. No. The wish to go to the forest now is evidence of failure to understand the idea of the F.P.O.
2. The principle of the Jewish Partisan Organization is social and national, to organize the struggle of the Jews and to defend our lives and our honour.
3. To go to the forests at this time would mean the search for individual security, individual escape, just as hiding in a *maline* means search for individual security.
4. We will go to the forests, but as the result of battle. When we have carried out our purpose here, we will take with us as great a number of Jews as possible and continue our struggle against the murdering occupier as part of the partisan movement.
5. It is only through battle, and as a result of our resistance, that we shall be able to save large numbers of Jews." [53]

There were, however, dissenting voices in the F.P.O. leadership, and some of its members refused to approve the command's decisions. Those who objected to this officially adopted F.P.O. strategy claimed that fighting the Nazis inside the ghetto was doomed from the outset to failure. They motivated their position with several convincing arguments. First, they claimed, that it was delusive to believe that the non-Jewish residents of Vilnius and vicinity will become involved in the Jewish anti-Nazi struggle. Moreover, it would be difficult to inflict any significant loses and damage to the overwhelming forces of the enemy. And, finally, few Jews, if any, could be saved in open combat with the German military and security forces in the ghetto. Instead, they asserted that fighting the Nazis in the forest, in a Jewish national partisan detachment, would be a struggle for Jewish honour. It could save the lives of hundreds, if not thousands, Jewish youngsters who in time of need could come back from the forest and assist the ghetto Jews in their struggle in the city.[54]

The above F.P.O. resolutions, adopted in the early spring of 1943, at the time of relative peace in the ghetto, were important political documents, rather than practical guides for military action. They obviously bore the mark of Witenberg's determination to fight the Nazis inside the ghetto, and his belief that the city communist underground, and friendly gentiles in the city, will be able and willing to provide practical support to the ghetto fighters. In the summer of 1943, however, the situation changed drastically. Witenberg was dead, murdered by the Nazis, and the communist underground organization in Vilnius was in a shambles. In these new circumstances it was requisite for the F.P.O. to set its priorities straight and redefine its mode of operation. Unfortunately, the cumbersome organizational structure of the F.P.O., the multi-party composition of its leadership, and, perhaps, the lack of experience in dealing with situations of extreme complexity, hindered its ability to make quick decisions, or change its course of action on short notice. After the surrender of Wittenberg, and the departure of Glazman, Ziskovitsh joined the command staff of the F.P.O. Kaplan, Madesker, and Ziskovitsh were appointed battalion commanders, and Reznik treasurer.[55]

The F.P.O. was a closely knit organization, and most members were admitted on the basis of political and party affiliation rather than by the natural selection of those who were most fit for military combat duty. Personal contacts and political connections, rather than life experience, military training and combat usefulness, determined the hierarchical structure of this organization. The political multi-party essence of the F.P.O. made it difficult for the organization to assume the general leadership of all young people in the ghetto. Unaffiliated armed youths, with no political contacts, who were ready and willing to fight, were in many instances denied the chance of getting involved in organized anti-Nazi activity. In 1942, at the early stages of operation, secrecy and loyalty were of utmost importance and the detachment of the F.P.O. from the masses was justified. But even in the summer of 1943, when the existence of an armed resistance movement in the ghetto was no longer a secret to any Jew in the ghetto, the F.P.O. continued its policy of isolation. The events early in September 1943, which were a prelude to the final liquidation of the ghetto, proved that the F.P.O. was unable to assess the situation objectively and incapable, or unwilling, either to open the gates of the ghetto and move into the forest, or put its combat regulations into practice.

Wednesday, 1 September 1943, marked the beginning of the end of the ghetto in Vilnius. At dawn the ghetto was surrounded by Nazi troops. Estonian SS-men entered the ghetto and began abducting people on the streets, intending to round up some 5,000 men and women for deportation to concentrations camps in Estonia. When the F.P.O. command realized that the ghetto was surrounded it decided not to surrender without a fight, and issued a mobilization order, and a Proclamation to the ghetto residents. Khvoinik and Ziskovitsh suggested that military action be taken immediately, Kovner, instead, insisted that action be delayed until the situation clarifies. The F.P.O. Manifesto called,

"Jews, Prepare for Armed resistance!
The German and Lithuanian hangmen have reached the gates of the ghetto.
They will murder us all.
They will take us, group by group, through the gates.
That is how they took.... our brothers, sisters, fathers, mothers, our children.
That is how they took tens of thousands away to their death.
But we will not go!
We will not let them take us like animals to slaughter.
Jews prepare for armed resistance!
Do not believe the false assurances of the murderers, do not believe the words of the traitors. Whoever is taken through the gate of the ghetto has only one road - Ponary. And Ponary is death.
Jews we have nothing to lose.
Death is certain. Who can still believe that he will survive when the murderers kill systematically? The hand of the hangman will reach out to each of us. Neither hiding nor cowardice will save lives.
Only armed resistance can save our lives and honour.
Brothers, it is better to fall in battle in the ghetto than to be led like sheep to Ponary.
Know that in the ghetto there is an organized Jewish force which will rise up with arms in its hands.
Rise up for the armed resistance! ....
Those who have no arms get hold of an axe. Those who haven't an

axe take hold of an iron bar or cudgel!....
Strike the murderers! ....
Long live liberty! Long live armed resistance!
Death to the murderers!" [56]

The Proclamation was signed by the F.P.O. (United Partisan Organization) Command Staff.

The situation in the ghetto on 1 September 1943 was, however, more complicated than the leaders of the F.P.O. anticipated. Even before the F.P.O. managed to gather its members and distribute the concealed weapons, most still unarmed fighters of one battalion, which gathered at Szpitalna (Ligoniniu) Street, were surrounded by German and Estonian soldiers and removed with no resistance from the ghetto for transportation to Estonia. The F.P.O. leadership was shocked, but could do little to alleviate the situation. This incident not only reduced the combat capability of the F.P.O., but also exposed the inadequate level of intelligence, and the lack of communication between different members and units, in the organization.

The headquarters of the F.P.O. were located on 6 Strashun (currently 4 Zemaitijos) Street. This three storey structure was situated at the end of a street which was separated from the city by a high brick wall. Most F.P.O. forces, under the command of Aba Kovner, were assembled there. It appeared that the F.P.O. was ready to act. According to Ruzka Korchak the initial plan stipulated that F.P.O. members were supposed to open fire at the Nazis, entering the ghetto, from a position near the ghetto gate, currently located at 11 Rudninku (Rudnicka) Street.[57] By 6 A.M., however, the ghetto was full of Germans who entered the ghetto unhindered. The building of 11 Rudninku (Rudnicka) Street was inside the ghetto, but most of its windows were facing the street outside the ghetto, and that made it possible to attack the Nazis even before they have entered the ghetto gates.

The F.P.O. leadership devised then a new plan of action according to which the alleged barricade at 6 Strashun Street was to be the main centre of defence. In order to protect the approaches to 6 Strashun Street it was decided to man two defence outposts at 7 and 8 Strashun Street, and two frontal combat positions in the houses at 12 and 15 of the same street. The main objective of the fighters, placed at 12 Strashun

Street, was to block the entrance of the Nazis into the street and protect the F.P.O. headquarters from any unexpected attack. For additional security a machine-gun unit with several fighters was placed on the balcony of 7 Strashun Street which overlooked and exposed to fire the entrance into the street. The F.P.O. command envisaged that after the initial resistance of its fighters the whole ghetto population will become involved in battle. If it transpired, however, that it would be impossible to defend the position at 6 Strashun Street, the F.P.O. leaders would order the ghetto wall to be blown up and open the road for escape into the city. [58]

The new challenge to the safety of the ghetto engendered a tacit agreement between the chief of the Jewish police and the F.P.O. according to which the FPO was not to undertake any resistance activity unless the Germans approached its fighting positions. [59] The Jewish police promised to make a concentrated effort to deliver the required number of people for deportation, and it tried hard to divert the attention of the Nazis from Strashun Street, making thus sure that they did not approach the F.P.O. main barricade. However, "when only 600 men and women had been arrested by the Jewish police by evening, the Germans and Estonians again entered the ghetto." [60]

It did not take long before the Germans reached Strashun Street, and approached the number 12 structure. When the Germans appeared in sight the resistance fighters opened fire. The Germans returned fire with automatic weapons, and blew up the building. The machine-gun, stationed on the balcony of 7 Strashun Street, remained silent and no support for the fighters at 12 Strashun Street followed. Many years later, Elchanan Magid, one of the fighters at the above machine-gun position, asserted that he was able to see how the Germans were placing explosives at 12 Strashun Street and he was ready to shoot, but there was no order and he relented. [61]

Morton Shames who was allegedly one of those in charge of the machine-gun at the balcony of 7 Strashun Street later declared that

"from my position ... I could see from quite a distance two soldiers carrying a box of explosives and after a while running away empty handed. Some of my fighters expressed impatience and asked for orders to shoot. But I refused. I understood very well their desire of revenge no matter what the consequences will be. But I could not afford to be carried away by emotions. It was clear to me at that moment there was nothing we could gain by shooting. The two soldiers were too far away and in my estimation out of range. I also thought that the sound of the machine-gun could very well provoke the Gestapo to destroy the ghetto itself." [62]

It appears today that the machine-gunners, at the balcony of 7 Strashun Street, did not open fire because there was no order from the F.P.O. command to shoot, and because in order to save bullets they were supposed to fire only from close range and when there would be many Nazis in sight.[63]

The rubble of the blown up and demolished house at 12 Strashun Street covered the street and made it difficult the passage to the F.P.O. headquarters. After the explosion the Germans did not attempt to pursue the surviving resistance fighters, and soon after the incident at 12 Strashun Street they withdrew from the ghetto.

The next day, 2 September 1943, few Germans or Estonians appeared in the ghetto, leaving the job of rounding up Jewish men and women to the Jewish police. On 5 September 1943 the deportation action was completed and temporary calm set in. The next day, on 6 September 1943, the FPO came out with a new plan of action. Its main goal was now to leave the ghetto and move into the woods. However, it asserted that if instead of rounding up people for transportation to working camps, the Nazis decided to liquidate the ghetto completely, members of the F.P.O. would stop their escape to the forest, and, if necessary, fight the aggressor.[64] The F.P.O. stated clearly that it will go into action only when according to its estimation it will be the beginning of the end, "yet it will not go into action to defend the life of any individual Jew." [65]

That was, of course, another well meaning pronouncement, but the F.P.O. lacked the resolve to act. Its leaders observed how the Germans emptied the ghetto step by step, but they still believed that the ghetto might survive. Two weeks later the ghetto was liquidated anyway, but instead of being buried under the rubble of blown up and demolished buildings, as it would inexorably happen in the case of an uprising inside the ghetto, most ghetto residents were shipped to labour and concentration camps where there was still some hope and a chance of survival for the young. In an account written in March 1944 N. Reznik, one of the members of the F.P.O. command staff, summarized the situation in the ghetto, that ominous September, in a dispassionate and self-critical manner. He asserted that

"on 1 September 1943, when the Germans and Estonian police entered the Vilnius ghetto, the shrunken F.P.O., taken by surprise, tried to mobilize for defence, but half the units could not reach their arsenal and others simply fled. Some resisters waited at their preselected bit of ghetto terrain for Germans to arrive, but no armed encounter of significance took place. The F.P.O. did not impede the Germans in their work of rounding up some eight thousand Jews - about two thirds of the ghetto - for deportation. That F.P.O. failure convinced the members that their most prudent course would be to leave the remnant ghetto. Within days about two hundred young people succeeded in joining the partisans in the woods."[66]

On 23 September 1943, when the Germans announced the final liquidation of the ghetto, the FPO command, together with its still remaining fighters in the ghetto, in total close to a hundred men and women, managed to escape from the ghetto. They made use of the complicated route through the city sewer system which they entered in the ghetto and exited in a safe and secret location outside the ghetto. This route was kept secret not only from unaffiliated ghetto youths, but from the general F.P.O. membership as well. When unaffiliated young Jews in the ghetto sensed that the end of the ghetto was near, many were desperate to leave and tried to follow F.P.O. members on their way of escape. The F.P.O. command, however, issued a strict order that no individual, who did not belong to the organization, should be permitted to join the F.P.O. fighters on their way to the forest.[67] The order from the F.P.O. headquarters was unequivocal. No F.P.O. member was allowed to bring along to the secret exit from the ghetto, and help escape, even one's family members.[68] Today, surviving members of the F.P.O. leadership deny such accusations and claim that anyone able and willing could leave the ghetto before its liquidation.[69] The situation in the ghetto, however, was in those days very complicated and there is enough evidence to suggests that the F.P.O. did not do enough to assist unaffiliated youths in their desire to escape to the forest.[70] The escape of Witenberg's son, however, was arranged by the F.P.O. command and he left the ghetto

together with the FPO fighters through the sewers system.[71]   Most
F.P.O. members, who escaped from the ghetto that day, managed to
reach the Rudninku forests where they joined the pro-Soviet partisan
detachments.

Today, there is no precise information as to the number of Jews
from the ghetto in Vilnius who did manage to escape from the ghetto,
in time, and join the partisan units in the Narocz forests in Belorussia or
the Rudninku forests in Lithuania. According to some sources, approximately 500 Jews from the Vilnius ghetto reached the forest. This figure
had been even confirmed in the Moscow newspaper *Pravda*, the official
organ of the USSR Communist Party Central Committee. Other, probably more reliable, sources suggest that the number of Jewish partisans
from Vilnius was approximately 360.[72]

One might wonder today why did the F.P.O. not impede the
Germans in their work of rounding up thousands of Jews for deportation when it was clear to most sober individuals in the ghetto that the
days of the ghetto in Vilnius were numbered. It is possible to presume
that the lack of resolve to act was caused by the unexpected departure
of Witenberg who was apparently the most courageous and determined,
albeit somewhat idealistic, individual in the F.P.O. command. There was
no question that if attacked by the Germans the F.P.O. would use its
arms in self-defence, but in given circumstances, full of unexpected sur-
prises, it preferred to wait, replacing its high sounding proclamations
with a pragmatic approach to life in which, in the end, their own survival
became their main objective.

One might also wonder today whether armed resistance within
the walls of the Vilnius ghetto was indeed the best course of action. The
decision to fight the Nazis in the ghetto was not only a military decision,
but an ethical one as well. The more so since most ghetto residents
opposed it. It is clear today that "the F.P.O. did not take the offensive
because of the... unanswerable moral question that plagued the ghetto....
what if it was not the final liquidation, and was it right to endanger and
expose all ghetto inhabitants against their wishes."[73]

It is clear today that the military strategy of the F.P.O. which
envisaged, as late as in the summer of 1943, the possibility of armed
resistance within the ghetto, was short-sighted. And yet, one could hardly

blame the F.P.O. for its failure to initiate an armed confrontation with the overwhelming forces of the enemy. Moreover it is highly questionable whether an uprising, staged by the underground resistance movement in the Vilnius ghetto, would make possible the survival of more Jews than in concentration camps. Y. Arad summarized the dilemma of the F.P.O. succinctly and to the point. To the question "Why the Uprising Did not take Place?" he replied that "the F.P.O. blamed the Jews for not joining their call for resistance when in fact they alone, and only they, could precipitate the bloody confrontation which no one wanted, not the Jews in the ghetto nor the F.P.O., everyone wanted to live and hoped for survival."[74]

The surrender of Witenberg and the failure of the F.P.O. to act is a major tragedy rather than a shameful defeat. There is no doubt that had the F.P.O. not attempted the impossible of combining the defence of a defenceless ghetto with the notion of fighting as partisans in the forest, many more young Jews could have been saved. "Yet although they had failed, they had failed tragically and not ignominiously."[75]

The F.P.O. failed to live up to its proclaimed objectives, but it gave hope, dignity, and support to many otherwise downtrodden people in the ghetto. Moreover, by conducting acts of sabotage in Nazi occupied Lithuania it inflicted much damage to Nazi military installations and the institutions of the German civil administration in the city. Vilnius was the first city where

> "defying the traditional Jewish leadership, a new generation of leaders, in their twenties and thirties, had the moral and intellectual courage to admit to themselves that the extermination of European Jewry was one of the chief war aims of Nazi Germany, and that the only Jewish answer to it must be to die fighting. Vilnius thus became the birth place of the idea and deed of armed resistance and from there it was carried to Bialystok and Warsaw where it saw its fulfilment."[76]

Just as before the war when Wilno was the centre of Jewish religious, cultural, and political life in Eastern and Central Europe, under Nazi occupation Vilnius became the spiritual centre of anti-Nazi resistance. The resistance leaders and members of the Jewish underground in the Vilnius ghetto informed Jewish communities and educated individual Jews in Nazi occupied regions about the imminent danger of

destruction, and encouraged them to escape, resist, and not submit without a struggle. After their escape from the devastated ghetto in Vilnius
most members of the Jewish ghetto resistance movement waged successful battle with the Nazi enemy in the ranks of Soviet partisan detachments. Moreover, after the liberation from Nazi oppression some
continued their struggle in the ranks of the Soviet army, while many
others joined in the struggle for the independence of Israel.

CHAPTER THREE:

Yechiel (Ilya) Sheinbaum and the Second Fighting Organization

Yechiel (Ilya) Sheinbaum

Yechiel (Ilya) Sheinbaum and the Second Fighting Organization

THE F.P.O. WAS THE LARGEST AND BEST ORGAN-
ized underground resistance body in the Vilnius ghetto, but it was not
the only one. There were also other groups, of different sizes and various political stripes, the members of which, however, were not motivated by immediate ideological or political considerations. Their first choice
was survival, and if that was impossible then, at least, death with dignity.
Members of these groups discarded the notion of confrontation with
the Nazi enemy inside the ghetto because they believed that it was a futile
endeavour . Their main objective was to leave the ghetto as soon as possible and, at the first opportunity, join pro-Soviet partisans in the Lithuanian and Belorussian forests. In their estimation that would make possible
the survival of many more young Jews, inflicting, at the same time, greater
damage to the Nazi enemy. Only in extreme circumstances, when there
would be no way out from the ghetto, were they prepared to join the
other resistance fighters and face the Nazi enemy within the walls of the
ghetto.

Next to the F.P.O. the so-called Second Fighting Organization was
the most important underground resistance organization in the ghetto. It
was composed of a number of diverse resistance groups the members
of which for different reasons could not join the F.P.O. The history of
this organization is closely linked with the name of Yechiel Sheinbaum
who was both the spiritual and military leader of the this resistance body.

Sheinbaum was one of those who believed that those who intended to fight the Germans, and their collaborators, within the ghetto walls were doomed, and he urgently called for an early departure of all young people from the ghetto to the forest. Sheinbaum was the first, in the Vilnius ghetto, to open fire at the Nazis who were rounding up Jews for deportation to concentration and death camps. He was also the first, and perhaps the only one, to fall in open battle with the overwhelming forces of the enemy inside the Vilnius ghetto.

Yechiel Sheinbaum was not a native or pre-war resident of Wilno. He was born on 2 December 1914 in the Russian city of Odessa (currently Ukraine). During the First World War, when Yechiel was two years old, his parents moved to the city of Kowel. Between the two world wars the city was under Polish jurisdiction. Currently it is located in the western regions of independent Ukraine. When Yechiel was three years old his mother died from consumption at the age of twenty-eight. The young Yechiel was brought up by his paternal grandmother and eventually moved in with her. Yechiel's relationship with his father was not an easy one. His father remarried and Yechiel disliked his step-mother. Moreover, from his early youth Yechiel was involved in Zionist activity while his father was an anti-Zionist.

Having received his basic education in a *"Tarbut"* school, in which the language of instruction was Hebrew, Yechiel became a member of the Zionist youth organization *"Hehalutz Hatsair (Dror)"* in Kowel. At the age of sixteen he joined the so-called *Hakhshara*, a special youth camp to prepare those who intended to settle in a *kibbutz*, or a communal farming settlement, in Palestine. In the mid 1930s Yechiel was conscripted for service in the Polish Army. Despite poor health he worked hard and managed to reach the rank of an officer. After his release from the army Sheinbaum returned to Kowel and joined there a Zionist *kibbutz*. By that time he was already a recognized Zionist youth leader. In 1938 Yechiel moved to the Polish city of Lodz and joined there the Borochov *kibbutz*. His main objective was to prepare for the forthcoming journey to Palestine. Yechiel's departure, however, was delayed because of his responsibilities as a Zionist educator and youth leader in Poland. Indeed, one of his older sisters did manage to escape from Poland, before the beginning of the Second World War, and survive the war and the Holocaust in Palestine.

The German invasion of Poland, on 1 September 1939, dashed

Sheinbaum's plans. The city of Lodz was soon occupied by the *Wehrmacht*, while his hometown Kowel fell into the hands of the Soviets. In these new circumstances, when Jews in Nazi occupied Poland anticipated Nazi persecution and tyranny, Sheinbaum was charged by his organization with the responsibility of arranging the escape of members of the organization from Nazi occupied Lodz to Kowel. Under Soviet rule, however, no Zionist activity was possible in Kowel and, therefore, Sheinbaum became involved in the transfer of his people from Kowel to Vilnius. In October 1939 Vilnius was transferred by the Soviets to the jurisdiction of Lithuania, and became the capital of independent Lithuania. In Vilnius there was still a possibility to conduct Zionist activity, and there was still some hope to move from Lithuania to Palestine. In Vilnius Sheinbaum joined a *kibbutz* composed mostly of Zionist refugees from Nazi occupied Poland. These refugees, including Sheinbaum, did not intend to remain in Vilnius for long. Their main purpose was to get ready and leave Vilnius, as soon as possible, in the direction of Palestine. Some Zionists from Vilnius were successful in this endeavour. They managed to leave Vilnius before Nazi occupation and were lucky to reach Palestine in due time. Prior to Sheinbaum's intended departure, however, Soviet guards stopped a group of young Zionists from Vilnius, at the Soviet-Lithuanian border, and the small escape window to freedom was unexpectedly shut.

The incorporation of Lithuania into the USSR, in the summer of 1940, changed the existing situation drastically. All forms of Jewish national and social life in Lithuania were forbidden by the Soviets, and the activity of all Zionist associations was abruptly terminated. Under Soviet rule the Zionist *kibbutz* in Vilnius was forced to cease operation and Yechiel was impelled to accept the position of an electrical engineer in Vilnius. In November 1940 he married in Vilnius, Pesia Zlotnik, a fellow Zionist refugee from Poland whom he previously met in the *kibbutz* in Lodz.

The German invasion of the USSR, on 22 June 1941, did not shatter Sheinbaum's Zionist ideals, but it destroyed all practical possibilities to put them into action.[1] Now there was little room for long term plans, because the main objective of daily existence was physical and emotional survival. And yet, from the first day of Nazi occupation Sheinbaum ruled out surrender without a fight. On the sixth of September 1941, when Yechiel and his wife, together with other Vilnius Jews, were driven into the ghetto Yechiel told Pesia that they have to find a way to escape into the forest. Sheinbaum was aware of the extent of Nazi ferocity and the danger it posed to each individual Jew under Nazi occupation. The above notwithstanding Sheinbaum was convinced that he will manage to escape murder. At the same time, he urged the Jews not to submit to the Nazi occupier and to fight when there was no chance to escape. The Jews next to him, in the marching column, suspected that he was crazy.[2] Indeed, early in September 1941 few Jews believed that they were all doomed, and that the Germans were capable of the horrid crimes later committed by them.

From the early days in the ghetto the difficult conditions of life forced Sheinbaum to accept a job in the city. He worked as an electrician in a German unit. At work he was always intense and exasperated. He resented his slavery and hated the Germans in charge. One of the German overseers at work told Sheinbaum's Jewish fellow workers that "we do not like him [Sheinbaum]. He never utters a word, he never smiles, and there is hatred in his eyes. I will kick him out."[3] Work in the German unit in the city was, at that time, indispensable for Sheinbaum since it provided him with the necessary means for immediate physical survival, but his main interests and concerns were of a political, social, and military nature.

From the day the ghetto was established Sheinbaum devoted most of his free time to Zionist activity, and soon he began gathering and organizing the work of the Zionist youth group "*Dror*." In the pre-war years the main objective of the members of "*Dror*" was to move to Palestine. In ghetto conditions organized anti-Nazi armed resistance became their primary goal, and the forest was to serve, in a sense, as a temporary replacement for their final destination of Palestine. In the winter of 1941-1942 Yechiel's group consisted of some twenty youths. In the ghetto the resistance philosophy of "*Dror*" affected little its basic Zionist ideological tenets. "*Dror*", however, departed somewhat from its former organizational precepts, and was ready now to accept into its ranks a number of politically uncommitted youngsters who rejected the idea of fighting with the oppressor in the ghetto, and wanted to move into the forest.

In the spring of 1942 various underground groups sought to consolidate all resistance activity in the ghetto, and contacts between Sheinbaum's group and the F.P.O. were established. At one point

Sheinbaum and his people considered joining the F.P.O., but negotiations conducted in the summer of 1942 produced no results. The F.P.O. was prepared to admit new members as individuals, while Sheinbaum insisted on retaining his group's identity within the general F.P.O. framework. He wanted his group to become an affiliate of the F.P.O. with a separate membership.

In the spring of 1942 another underground resistance group which was called the *Kamfsgruppe*, or Battle Group, was formed in the ghetto. It included in its ranks a number of mature individuals with former army service experience, some Zionists-Revisionists, as well as several Jewish ghetto policemen. The *Kamfsgruppe* was originally composed of three semi-independent groups of different sizes. The central command was made up of some twenty people, including the leaders of these different groups. Members of the Battle Group were mostly individuals who for different reasons could not, or refused to, join the F.P.O. Some did not belong to any political group affiliated with the F.P.O. Others disagreed with the objectives and mode of operation of the F.P.O. Still others had personal disagreements with members of the F.P.O. leadership. Finally there were those who knew nothing about the existence of the F.P.O. altogether. Among the most prominent members of the Battle Group were the head of a Jewish police precinct in the ghetto, Nathan Ring, Dr. Leo Bernstein, Shlomo Brand and Borka Freedman.

In the winter of 1942-1943 Sheinbaum's group and the Battle Group agreed to merge, forming the so-called Second Fighting Organization under the leadership of Yechiel. The unification of Sheinbaum's original group with the *Kamfsgruppe*, with Yechiel as the head of this combined new organization, brought together Sheinbaum's Zionist idealism and perseverence with the military expertise, pragmatic approach, and political connections of some members of the *Kamfsgruppe*. According to Sheinbaum's personal and political friends, people who knew him well, he was well organized, determined, straight forward, and strong willed. Similarly, his commitment to Zionism and the cause of Israel, and his devotion to his ideological associates who followed him was steadfast. Sheinbaum was respected by most people he came in touch with, and despite some political differences with members of the *Kamfsgruppe* Sheinbaum was chosen to lead the Second Fighting Organization. His complete dedication to the cause of this newly formed resistance body was never in doubt.

The new unified organization continued to grow and, in the winter-spring of 1943, it was joined by a number of diverse independent youth groups. A group of young people, who managed to survive the destruction of the ghetto in Grodno, turned up in the Vilnius ghetto and joined the Second Fighting Organization. Similarly, a group of youths from small towns in the vicinity of Vilnius who managed to escape the mass murder which   destroyed all Jewish communities in the Lithuanian countryside joined the Second Fighting Organization. Members of the Zionist group "*Akiva*," active in the peat digging camp in Biala Waka, were also accepted into the organization.

Moshe Kalchheim, one of the members of "*Akiva*" who joined the Second Fighting Organization, described Sheinbaum as a handsome, attractive, and charming individual. Yechiel exhibited exceptional composure in extreme situations. "The spirit of struggle was in him always aflame. He believed in his chosen path without reservations. He was born to lead people, and he inspired his subordinates with faith, and readiness for sacrifice."[4]

By September 1943 the Second Fighting Organization was composed of two battalions with a total membership of over 200 fighters. Three groups of five members in each formed a platoon, and four-five platoons formed a battalion. At first the organization obtained radio information news in the city and smuggled it into the ghetto. Later the Second Fighting Organization managed to instal its own radio receiver in the ghetto and distributed the radio news among its members. As early as in the spring of 1942, Sheinbaum managed to establish contacts with Polish sympathizers in the city, and since the spring of 1943 he was in touch with Soviet partisans in the Narocz forests.[5]

It was well known in the ghetto that the A.K. (Polish Home Army) was staunchly anti-Soviet. At one point the Germans even negotiated with the A.K. with the purpose of engaging them in the struggle against the pro-Soviet partisans in the Vilnius region. Initially the local A.K. agreed to assist the Nazis in their war against the Soviet partisans, in the end, however, the Head Command of the A.K. forbade such action.[6] And yet, according to contemporary Polish sources, the A.K. assisted the Jewish ghetto underground. Thus, a member of the A.K. Jadwiga Dudzcowna, established a contact with Sheinbaum and supported the Jewish resistance movement in many different ways. She assisted with the acquisition of arms; she travelled to Warsaw to establish contacts with Jewish underground resistance fighters in the Warsaw ghetto. Occasionally, she would even enter the ghetto in Vilnius to take out Jewish children and find for them safe shelter in catholic nunneries.[7]

Initially the F.P.O. was not happy with the proliferation of a variety of independent resistance groups in the ghetto, and it tried hard to keep all underground resistance activity in the ghetto under its control. The F.P.O. leaders feared that perchance some inexperienced young Jews might be caught by the Germans in the process of trying to smuggle weapons into the ghetto, and pose thus a grave danger to the whole underground resistance operation in the ghetto.

When the F.P.O. had learned about the existence of a second armed resistance organization in the ghetto it made a concentrated effort to undermine its activity. This task was assigned to the F.P.O. intelligence unit. According to Isaac Kowalski, a member of this unit, the duties of this intelligence body included, among others, the task of obtaining information concerning the Nazi extermination plans of the Jews in Vilnius. The F.P.O. was also eager to receive all available information regarding the attitude of the Jewish ghetto leaders to the underground resistance organizations in the ghetto. The F.P.O. leadership was particularly interested in the practical measures which the Jewish ghetto leaders were planning to apply in their dealings with the resistance movement in the ghetto. J. Glazman, the head of the F.P.O. intelligence unit, entrusted the F.P.O. member Isaac Kowalski with the assignment to infiltrate the Second Fighting Organization, learn about its activity, and report immediately back to Glazman about his findings. Kowalski, who was well acquainted with some members of the *Kamfsgruppe*, had no difficulty in joining the Second Fighting Organization. He spied for a while on the activity of this organization, and reported back to Glazman about his findings.

Soon after Glazman was provided by Kowalski with the information about the Second Fighting Organization, "the U.P.O. [F.P.O.] staff was called together in a special session and decided to take drastic steps toward abolishing the group which endangered the entire activity of the U.P.O." The F.P.O. suspected that the *Kamfsgruppe* was a tool of Gens, and it decided to do everything in its power to discourage its activity.

Originally, Jacob Gens, the head of the ghetto, was familiar with the operations of the *Kamfsgruppe* and clandestinely supported its activities.

Approached by N. Ring, however, Gens categorically refused to become openly involved in any underground activity out of fear of his deputy, S. Desler, who, in his estimation, was a Gestapo agent. After the F.P.O. leadership learned from Kowalski about the activities of the Battle Group, and its connections with Gens, "it was decided [by the F.P.O.] that Chiene Borowski, our 'ambassador' to the Judenrat, was to visit Dessler and inform him that Gens regarded him as a dangerous Gestapo man."[8] When, after the visit of Borowska to Desler, some representatives of the *Kamfsgruppe* approached Gens again, he was furious and refused to have anything to do with them. He obviously did not suspect that his opinion of Desler as a Gestapo agent was passed on to the latter by one of the F.P.O. leaders, and he evidently surmised that this was the job of some members of the *Kamfsgruppe*.

The conflicts and enmity between different resistance organizations in the ghetto notwithstanding, attempts to unify all underground activity in the ghetto, with the purpose of forming a single fighting organization, with a joint command, persisted. Negotiations between the F.P.O. and the Second Fighting Organization resumed in May 1943 and continued in the spring and summer. The F.P.O. was represented in these negotiations by Y. Witenberg and Ch. Borowska, and the Second Fighting Organization by Y. Sheinbaum, Sh. Brand, and L. Bernstein. There are today many conflicting accounts about the results of these negotiations. Dov Levin suggests that the negotiations were successful, and that "an almost complete coalition was effected between the F.P.O. and the Yechiel organization."[9] Y. Arad, on the other hand, asserts that despite the agreement to cooperate and coordinate action, the alleged union between the F.P.O. and the Yechiel group "did not lead to the fusion and unification of the two organizations."[10]

Initially the F.P.O. demanded that members of the Second Fighting Organization join as individuals rather than as a group, give up their weapons for safekeeping in the F.P.O. arms repositories, and stop acquiring arms. Members of the Second Organization would lose thus their former group identity, and those accepted into the F.P.O. would be assigned as individuals into regular F.P.O. detachments. The Second Fighting Organization, instead, was prepared to join the F.P.O. as a separate battalion, retaining, at the same time, the rights to admit new members and acquire arms. It expected also to have its representative on the joint command staff of this new unified resistance organization.

In the end the F.P.O. was forced to compromise and agreed to most conditions set by the Sheinbaum group. It was agreed that after the F.P.O. will check the membership list of the Second Fighting Organization, the latter will join the new united partisan organization as an independent battalion. It will retain the right to admit new members, but it will have to report to the F.P.O. about any personnel changes and provide a list of new members admitted. In addition the Second Fighting Organization would continue to exercise control over the arms in possession of its members, and would retain its right to acquire new weapons. A liaison between the commands of the two organizations was to be established, and when important decisions were to be taken by the F.P.O. command staff, representatives of the Second Organization were to be present at the meeting.[11] Yechiel Sheinbaum was appointed representative of the Second Fighting Organization to the F.P.O. command staff.

It appeared thus that the Second Fighting Organization became an affiliate of the F.P.O., but its priorities did not change and remained different from those established by the F.P.O. command. Ideological matters, in regard to combat inside the ghetto or withdrawal into the forest, were not covered by the agreement, and each side remained autonomous in this respect. The primary objective of the F.P.O. was still to confront the Nazi enemy inside the ghetto, while the Second Fighting organization continued to adhere to the philosophy of the forest, and regarded the strategy of fighting in the ghetto as absurd. The Yechiel fighters agreed, however, to take part in combat activity within the ghetto, if the situation, at a given time, warranted such action, and there would be no other choice.

The peaceful coordination of the activities of the F.P.O. and the Second Fighting Organization did not last long. The members of these two diverse organizations hardly had enough time to become well acquainted which each other when the strained situation in the ghetto soon put to a test the diverse philosophies and strategies of these two allegedly affiliated bodies. Indeed, by the time the agreement between the F.P.O. and the Second Fighting Organization was reached the Germans were already alerted to the fact that there were armed individuals in the Vilnius ghetto. Thus, as early as on 21 April 1943, a group of young armed Jews, members of the Battle Group, under the leadership of Borka Freedman, left the ghetto for the Rudninku forest. On their way they were encountered by a German military ambush and most Jewish fighters perished in battle.[12]

The Witenberg debacle in July 1943, which was followed by the confrontation of the Glazman group with the Nazis on the outskirts of the city, aggravated the situation further. There could have been no doubt, at that time, that these incidents reinforced Nazi suspicion that military resistance activity was brewing in the Vilnius ghetto, and that armed Jews in the ghetto have established contacts with Soviet partisans roaming the forests in the Lithuanian and Belorussian countryside. It was obvious to any well informed Jew in the ghetto that some preventive action by the German administration was to be expected at any moment.

The difference in the resistance philosophies of the F.P.O. leadership and Sheinbaum's group became increasingly evident early in August 1943 when the Germans initiated major deportation actions from the ghetto. The F.P.O. could not assess the situation objectively and continued to vacillate. It could not decide whether this was a prelude to the final liquidation of the ghetto, or just another deportation action. Yechiel's' group, on the other hand, was bent on leaving the ghetto regardless. Sheinbaum insisted that groups of young Jews should be sent into the forest without delay so that they could prepare a base for those who will be able to evade deportation and escape when the final liquidation of the ghetto will take place. The final test of the two divergent resistance strategies occurred unexpectedly and without advance warning. When, on 1 September 1943, a new massive deportation action was initiated by the Nazis, the Jewish fighters stationed at the school premises at 12 Strashun Street, and headed by Yechiel Sheinbaum, attacked the Germans, entering the Street.

Today, it is not difficult to infer that the 1- 4 September 1943 deportation action was a continuation of the round ups that started early in August. By that time, it was already clear even to any uninitiated ghetto resident that the Germans have already decided to empty the ghetto step by step, rather than in one shot. Being aware of the fact that there were armed Jews in the Vilnius ghetto, they lulled the ghetto administration into believing that the future of the ghetto was safe, and in the meantime, in order to avoid the possibility of armed resistance, they were removing all young and able-bodied man and women from the ghetto to concentration camps in Estonia and Latvia.

The retreat of the Germans from the ghetto, on 1 September 1943, after having blown up the building of 12 Strashun Street, without responding forcefully to the challenge of the Jewish fighters, was a clear sign that the Germans did not want to become involved in urban guerrilla warfare. Drawing on the experience of the uprising in the Warsaw ghetto, in the spring of 1943, they knew that it could take weeks before a ghetto uprising would be suppressed, and in the meantime it would tie-up German military manpower which was urgently needed, at that time, at the eastern front.

The history of the outpost on 12 Strashun Street is a special case in the resistance struggle in the Vilnius ghetto. That was the only place where the Nazis were greeted with fire, and, in that sense, the only expression of armed resistance in the ghetto. According to Mark Dworzecki, there were that day approximately forty fighters at 12 Strashun Street. Some twenty were members of the Second Fighting Organization, the others were from the group of Chaim Rubashov .[13] The real surname of the leader of the group that joined the fighters at 12 Strashun Street was Rubanowicz, rather than Rubashov. It was a group of unaffiliated youngsters, without any preconceived political notions, or ideological commitments. Its members sought means to organize, procure weapons, and leave the ghetto for the forest in order to join the pro-Soviet partisans as soon as possible.

On 1 September 1943, when the ghetto was surrounded by Nazi troops and a mass deportation action began, members of the Rubanowicz group refused to surrender without a fight and decided to approach the F.P.O. in order to join in the forthcoming battle. The leaders of the F.P.O. received Rubanowicz and his people coolly. They were prepared to admit to their organization some members of this group as individuals on condition that they give up their weapons allegedly for safekeeping in the general F.P.O. arms repositories. Since Rubanowicz refused this offer it was suggested to him that if members of his group wanted to participate in the struggle they should follow to 12 Strashun Street. There, they were told, were allegedly some fortifications manned by F.P.O. fighters. That was how Rubanowicz, and some 15-20 members of his group, turned up that ominous day at 12 Strashun Street. They hardly knew there anyone, but they soon realized that the man, standing at the front window in the school room that was facing Strashun Street, was older and more mature than most others, and that he was apparently in charge of the other fighters.[14] Indeed, this was Yechiel Sheinbaum, who by all accounts was appointed commander of this position.

The policy of the F.P.O. which provided that all unaffiliated armed youngsters who wanted to join this organization were required to give up their weapons for alleged safekeeping, without any assurances that they will ever get them back, is corroborated today by accounts of other unorganized ghetto fighters. Thus, Baruch Shub was an unaffiliated ghetto youngster who managed with great difficulty to obtain a gun in the city and smuggle it into the ghetto. On 1 September 1943, with some help of his friends who were members of the F.P.O., Shub succeeded in infiltrating the F.P.O. barricade at 6 Strashun Street. The same F.P.O. insiders sponsored later Shub's admission to this organization. In the end, however, Shub refused the offer to join the F.P.O. because, as he claimed, "I was required to give up my gun for safekeeping in the general F.P.O arsenal. I asked them [my friends] whether I will get my gun back whenever I will need it, and received no satisfactory reply."[15]

It was obvious that the price of admission to the F.P.O. was too high, by far. The F.P.O. leaders surely knew how difficult and dangerous it was to procure arms in the ghetto. They were also aware of the fact that without a reliable weapon membership in their organization was meaningless, particularly to those who were strangers, and had no former political ties, or ideological connections, with the leadership of that organization.

The resistance fighters who manned the defence position at 12 Strashun Street were the first to confront the German attack, but its fighters were poorly armed. Some had hand-guns, others only grenades or Molotov cocktails. Sheinbaum despatched an urgent request to the F.P.O. command, demanding automatic weapons and additional ammunition. He was promised by the F.P.O. leaders a machine-gun which failed, however, to arrive in due time.

There are today many conflicting reports describing the events at 12 Strashun Street. Some are realistic, truthful, and to the point. Others are in the realm of documentary fiction. The well known Yiddish poet and writer A. Sutskever, or I. Kowalski, for example, portray the affair in the language of heroic epos. Others do it in more restrained tones. In a book, published immediately after the war in Moscow, Sutskever wrote that

"when the Germans approached [12 Strashun Street]... a fire was opened from the barricade.... The Germans called for reinforcements, and hundreds of murderers arrived in the ghetto. They opened heavy fire at 12 Strashun Street. The commander, Sheinbaum, who stood at the window, firing at the Germans, was the first to fall dead into the arms of his comrades . The fighter Reizel Korchak took over the command. The Germans, who were faced with strong resistance, blew up the building. Close to a hundred people perished under the rubble." [16]

Isaac Kowalski, allegedly a member of both the F.P.O. and the Second Fighting Organization, who claims to have been on 1 September 1943 at 12 Strashun Street, describes his alleged valiant exploits and takes credit for recovering the gun and ammunition of Sheinbaum who has been shot dead by the Germans. Kowalski declares that he was assigned with twelve or thirteen other fighters to the post on 12 Strashun Street. When the Germans blew up the house across the street, at 15 Strashun Street, the commander Sheinbaum ordered

"to fire at the Gestapo demolition men in the street as they stood admiring the results of their work. Ilya [Yechiel] Sheinbaum ... threw a grenade into the group of Nazis outside. It was a direct hit. Those who were able to escape ran, but not for long. We saw them take dynamite sticks and run to our side of the building. We fired at them, but soon lost them from sight, for they took up positions at the walls of the building. For a while it was quite. Then we heard commands to mine and blow up the entire house. We tried to find positions from which we would be able to fire at them and prevent their action. Ilya Sheinbaum leaned slightly out of a window to see where the Gestapo men were. At that moment there was a shot from below. I ... saw Ilya falling. I ... could see no injuries... but I saw he was dead. Ruzka Korchak gave orders to jump from the back windows.... I was the last to jump.... I barely had time to recover from the shock of falling when I heard the tremendous explosion that turned the entire building into a smoking heap of rubble." [17]

According to Chaim Lazar, a member of the F.P.O.,

"the front position was in the school auditorium on 12 Straszun Street. A company of fighters was sent there, made up mainly of members of the Second Organization. (That same day the two organizations merged completely). Ilya Scheinbaum, a leader of the Second Organization and a former officer in the Polish Army, was chosen as commander of the position.... The F.P.O. commander was upset by the appointment. He wanted members of his own movement in command. At the last minute, he appointed as commander of the position Rozka Korczak, despite her lack of military knowledge, and made Scheinbaum her second-in-command. At dusk several Gestapo men and Estonian soldiers came to the ghetto, and together with Gens and a number of Jewish policemen, approached the house on 12 Straszun Street to conduct a search, having heard that a lot of Jews were hiding in the yard. Ilya Scheinbaum stood at the window and saw the Germans approaching the building. According to plan , he fired shots and threw a grenade. But the grenade did not explode. The Germans retreated momentarily, but then opened heavy fire on the position. A bullet struck Scheinbaum, killing him. Rozka, the commander of the position, gave no orders to the fighters. She ran to the headquarters and said that everything was in order at the position and did not relate what had happened. The fighters at the position were confused. They waited for instructions which did not come. Though they saw that the building was about to be blown up, they did not leave it.... Several fighters.... [and] dozens of Jewish tenants were buried under the rubble."[18]

In a book written earlier, jointly with L. Eckman, Ch. Lazar provides another version of the same events. He reports

"that the front position on Straszsuna 12 was commanded by Yehiel Sheinbaum. When the Germans were seen approaching, Sheinbaum fired the first shot. The Germans called in reserves, and soon hundreds of armed men streamed into the ghetto to attack the barricade. It was a bloody battle, and the Germans were repulsed in several frontal assaults. Then, at the crucial moment, Sheinbaum fell, his body riddled with bullets.... Reizel Korchak then took over the defence. The Germans soon received their reinforcements but could still make no headway. Failing to gain a foothold in frontal attacks, the Germans decided on a change of tactics. German troopers with loads of dynamite stole behind the Jewish position and mined the barricade and its foundations.... Many fighters whom the Germans could not subdue in open combat were struck down in the explosion."[19]

R. Korchak was one of the few members of the F.P.O. present that ominous day at 12 Strashun Street. In a book, originally published in 1946, she declared that Sheinbaum was appointed head of the position at 12 Strashun Street. He ordered that the fighters should open fire after him. When the Germans approached, Sheinbaum

> "gives an order and shoots first. We throw grenades from the windows in the direction of the approaching enemy. The enemy answers immediately with heavy fire. The first falls Sheinbaum, the commander of the position. The Germans move away fast, and there is no one to shoot at any more. Suddenly news arrive that the Germans intend to blow up the house. The group of fighters receives an order to withdraw and unite with the main forces on 6 Strashun Street.... All the block, where our position was located was blown up. We soon learned that the Germans removed their wounded from Strashun Street, and withdrew from the ghetto."[20]

Another author, Y. Arad, provides probably the most sober, succinct, albeit incomplete, account of the events described. At noon on 1 September 1943, he suggests,

> "the F.P.O. issued a proclamation to all ghetto inhabitants calling for armed resistance to deportation .... With the exception of a party of youngsters who joined the F.P.O. position on Straszun Street, the inhabitants [of the ghetto] did not respond to the call of an uprising .... The F.P.O. fighters, under the command of Scheinbaum, who were in the forward position at 12 Straszuna opened fire at the Germans. They returned fire with automatic weapons. Scheinbaum was killed instantly and the other combatants retreated to the main position at 6 Straszuna at nightfall. The Germans blew up the house at no. 12 and left the ghetto at nightfall."[21]

Pesia, Yechiel's wife, was next to him at 12 Strashun Street. Before the Germans appeared on the street, Yechiel told her that if they will survive this day they will leave for the forest in the night. They had established firm contacts with partisans in the nearby forests, but Yechiel refused to leave earlier, because he would not abandon members of his group who were still to remain in the ghetto.[22] It was clear that Sheinbaum's dedication to his comrades, those who followed and entrusted him with their fate, had no bounds. He was supposed to be the last to leave the ghetto, but fate willed differently. Instead he was the first to fall. Pesia recounts her experiences of that day:

"I was standing near Ilya. We opened the glass windows and the fighters took up positions at the windows. The few handguns and Molotov cocktails were distributed among them. Ilya was the first to shoot several times from his revolver .... some fighters threw several Molotov cocktails. The Germans were surprised - 'Jews are shooting,' and immediately returned heavy fire .... A bullet struck Ilya in the neck. I was next to him .... He asked me to load a second magazine, when I suddenly heard Ruzka [Korchak] scream to me in Polish 'look, Ilya fell.' Later I did not see her anymore around .... German bullets continued to hit the windows and walls. When Ilya fell our people stopped fighting. Confusion set in .... and the fighters started to leave. I begged them 'help me take Ilya.' I still believed that he was alive. I could not imagine that he died so fast. [Ilya was saying] 'the Germans will never take me alive.' When we stopped shooting the Germans approached the building to place explosives. I dragged Ilya to another room and put him on the floor between the school benches. I saw that he was already cold... dead ... I jumped [from the second floor] to the ground, then went up to the roof, and with other colleagues managed to get to 6 Strashun Street."[23]

Aba Kovner, the commander of the F.P.O., was at the time of the confrontation at 12 Strashun Street at the F.P.O. main barricade at 6 Strashun Street. When Ruzka Korchak arrived and reported about Sheinbaum's death, and the hostilities at 12 Strashun Street, Kovner was shaken but he did not blame Sheinbaum for his precipitous actions. Ruzka Korchak, on the other hand, defended her action of abandoning the remaining fighters at 12 Strashun Street by claiming that by ordering the retreat to the main barricade, before the school building at 12 Strashun Street was blown up, she saved the fighters from a certain death.[24] She failed, however, to note that only members of the F.P.O. were admitted to the 6 Strashun Street barricade, while all other fighters, including the members of the Rubanowicz group, remained in the street to ward for themselves.

The different accounts of the events that occurred on 1 September 1943 at 12 Strashun Street are mostly provided by participants in the anti-Nazi resistance movement in the Vilnius ghetto who survived the Holocaust. With the exception of Isaac Kowalski all others, cited above, settled after the war in the state of Israel. The divergent renditions of the same event by different authors illustrate that the political and ideological squabbling in the ghetto has been carried over, after the war, into a new arena. The subject today is no longer the theory and practice of ghetto anti-Nazi resistance, but rather the historical interpretation of our recent past. At a Conference on Manifestations of Jewish Resistance, which took place in April 1968 in Jerusalem, Shimon Wiesenthal (Vienna) urged the participants not to "avoid topics which may be unpleasant." He asserted that historical truth requires that we "explain that the lack of unity among Jews during the Holocaust period contributed to the magnitude of the calamity."[25] Indeed, it is obvious today to any student of Jewish anti-Nazi resistance in the Vilnius ghetto that ideological and political rivalry between different political factions and resistance organizations in the ghetto precluded the possibility of escape and survival of many able-bodied Jews in the Vilnius ghetto.

After the Germans withdrew from the ghetto the body of Yechiel was found lying on a heap of smouldering bricks. The next day a funeral was arranged for Sheinbaum at the Vilnius Jewish cemetery, but only two Jewish policemen were permitted to accompany the makeshift coffin. That was the last funeral at the Vilnius Jewish cemetery under Nazi rule. After the liberation of Vilnius from Nazi occupation Sheinbaum's surviving friends returned from the forest and erected a monument at the nameless grave of Yechiel. Recently a commemorative plaque was installed at the wall of 8 Zemaitijos Street (formerly 12 Strashun Street) in honour of Yechiel Sheinbaum and the F.P.O. fighters who allegedly manned the position and faced the Nazis with fire. No mention is made of the fact that the majority of those present at 12 Strashun Street, on 1 September 1943, were unaffiliated youngsters, and that Sheinbaum was the leader of the Second Fighting organization.

After the death of Sheinbaum Elchanan Magid was appointed leader of the Second Fighting Organization. The loose bond between the F.P.O. and the Second Fighting Organization was severed, and most members of the Yechiel group began to act independently. The new situation in the ghetto, after 1-4 September 1943, temporarily created appropriate conditions for attempts to escape from the ghetto unnoticed, and some

Seventy members of the Second Fighting Organization took advantage of this opportunity and left the ghetto without consulting the F.P.O." But even then, when the fate of the ghetto was for all practical purposes already sealed, the distinction between the mode of operation and the strategies of the F.P.O. and Sheinbaum's group was obvious. "During the liquidation of the ghetto, scores of unaffiliated young people pressed to join the F.P.O. members, preparing to leave for the forest through the sewers. The F.P.O. decided it had to stop them with the use of arms. The Yechiel [group], on the other hand, was able to allow a number of unaffiliated and unarmed young people to join their ranks in their flight to the Rudninku forest." [27]

When one compares today the different approaches of the F.P.O. and Sheinbaum's group to the major enigma of ghetto politics, expressed in the relationship of resistance and survival, one inadvertently arrives at the conclusion that no system or strategy was totally foolproof. The Holocaust was a calamity of extraordinary proportions, and the Nazi plague was equal to a natural disaster of the greatest magnitude. The oppressor was a skilled, brutal and experienced murderer, and there were no special prescriptions for individual Jewish survival. Hence, resistance whether inside the ghetto or in the forest, could not guarantee survival. And yet, one has to admit that the chances of survival were much better in partisan units in the forest, than fighting the Nazis inside the ghetto. Sheinbaum stated repeatedly that armed resistance inside the ghetto had no chance of success, and that it was self-deception to believe that rebellion in the ghetto could create an opportunity for the non-combatant mass to escape. The mass was doomed anyway, but hundreds, even thousands, young Jews could be saved in the forest. [28]

When the real test came, on 1 September 1943, the F.P.O. issued a manifesto to all inhabitants of the ghetto, calling for armed resistance to deportation. But what could the unarmed, exhausted from malnutrition, and frightened ghetto Jews do when most F.P.O. fighters, with all their arms and ammunition, were biding their time in the barricade at 6 Strashun Street. How could the F.P.O. expect the ghetto Jews to resist deportation when the F.P.O. itself did not resist it. Ironically, Joseph Glazman one of the main F.P.O. resistance ideologists who initially supported the idea of fighting the Germans inside the ghetto, was forced to flee from the ghetto several months before its liquidation. He joined the pro-Soviet partisans in the Narocz forest, and consequently perished there in battle. Yechiel Sheinbaum, on the other hand, who most vehemently opposed the notion of fighting the Nazis within the ghetto, was the first to open fire at the enemy inside the Vilnius ghetto, and the first to perish there in battle.

At a time when great numbers of Jews were brutally killed every day, and savage murder was as common to every Jew in the ghetto as life itself, the death of a single individual in the ghetto would usually pass unnoticed. But Sheinbaum acted heroically and his death was a tragedy of great proportions. Despite the fact that he was in constant opposition to fighting the Nazis inside the ghetto, he did not hesitate to confront the overwhelming forces of the enemy and, when it was needed, sacrifice his life defending the honour and dignity of the downtrodden Jews in the ghetto. Sheinbaum's death substantiated, in a sense, the predication that armed resistance to the Nazis inside the Vilnius ghetto would be a waste of energy and of Jewish lives. And yet, Sheinbaum's death was not totally in vain. Ironically, it helped save the lives of many other Jews, including those of his political adversaries.

When the Germans blew up the school structure at 12 Strashun Street, and retreated from the ghetto, the street was covered with rubble and the passage to the main F.P.O. barricade at 6 Strashun Street was temporarily blocked. Thus, an armed confrontation between the Nazis and the main F.P.O. forces, which would be fraught with terrible consequences for the whole ghetto, was avoided. Until the last moments of the ghetto's existence, however, the F.P.O. leaders continued to delude themselves that a revolt inside the ghetto could be staged indeed, and that the remaining Jews in the ghetto will join in battle. It appears thus that "the plans of the F.P.O. ended in tragic failure, for the organization not only failed to stage an armed revolt 'when the existence of the entire ghetto' was 'at stake,' but it was also unable to carry alongside the mass of the people and lead it in any kind of breakout towards the forest."[29]

Today, one should not blame the F.P.O. for its reluctance to join in a losing battle. It was always clear that fighting the Nazis inside the ghetto was suicidal, and that armed resistance within the ghetto was no panacea. Some Jews did survive the Holocaust because they resisted Nazi oppression with arms in hand, mostly in partisan units in the forest. Others survived precisely because they did not resist, and because there was no uprising in the ghetto. In fact, there were "many Hasidic rebbes ....[who]

believed that they were living through a period in which ... 'strict justice' prevailed. This judgement upon them, they believed, was dictated by Divine Providence, and accordingly was to be accepted out of love for God.''[30] Some other rebbes, however, disagreed with such statements, and advocated resistance to the Nazi enemy.

In some instances resistance within the walls of the ghetto could make sense. In situations when there was no way to retreat or escape, and no anti-Nazi partisan bases in the vicinity, a ghetto uprising could be the only dignified solution. Hence, the original strategy of the F.P.O., devised early in 1942, when there were no Soviet partisans in the region yet, was proper. At that time there was nowhere to hide, and it was almost impossible for any Jew by birth to conceal his true identity. Non-Jewish inhabitant of pre-war Poland had an uncanny ability of recognizing a Jew even in disguise, and in most instances they would betray the Jew to the German authorities. Furthermore, the forests in the vicinity of Vilnius were mostly controlled by the unfriendly Polish A.K., and Lithuanian security forces which collaborated with and supported the Nazi regime. Death lurked all over, and death with dignity was the only honourable choice. An uprising in the ghetto would certainly inflict some losses on the enemy, and perhaps create an opportunity for escape for the few who had hiding places in the city, but the Jewish masses, and most resistance fighters, would in the end succumb to the overwhelming forces of the Nazi enemy and perish.

The Warsaw ghetto uprising, and the heroism of the Jewish fighters there, inspired the members of the Jewish underground resistance in the Vilnius ghetto. The situation in Warsaw, however, was different from that in Vilnius. Warsaw was much farther from the front-line and the advancing Soviet army than Vilnius. Moreover, there were no forest in the vicinity of Warsaw full of pro-Soviet partisans. The Polish A.K., operating in the region of Warsaw, was in practical terms of little help to the struggling Jews in the Warsaw ghetto.

In the region of Vilnius, however, in the summer of 1943, the situation was different. Soviet partisan bases were located within reach of the city, and partisan commanders were sending emissaries to the ghetto, exhorting the leaders of the Jewish ghetto resistance movement to send young armed Jews to the forest with the purpose of joining pro-Soviet partisan detachments. In such circumstances there was no reason to provoke the Nazis and initiate a destructive war inside the ghetto. The more so since the general ghetto population opposed it, and there was no chance of succeeding anyway. True, the partisans in the forest were ready to accept only young armed people, but even unarmed Jews had a better chance of surviving in the forests and marshes of the regions, controlled by the partisans, than in a ghetto, or concentration camp, under constant Nazi siege.

CHAPTER FOUR:

Jacob Gens and the Ghetto Police

Jacob Gens

Jacob Gens and the Ghetto Police

JACOB GENS WAS ONE OF THE MOST CONTRO-
versial Jewish ghetto leaders in Nazi occupied Eastern Europe. According to some he ruled with an iron hand, and was "hated among
many Jews as the Nazi rulers themselves."[1] According to others "Gens
... was a thoroughgoing idealist ... [who] believed he could reach [his] ...
goal by a combination of accommodation and resistance."[2]

Jacob Gens was born on 1 April 1903 in Ilgvieciai, a small village in
the Siauliai district, in Lithuania. His father was a merchant of modest
means. Jacob was the oldest of four brothers, but had no sisters. According to the daughter of Gens, Ada Gensaite-Ustijanauskiene, under
tsarist rule the parents of Gens resisted Russification. They spoke well
Lithuanian and the Lithuanian national spirit reigned in their abode.[3]

Before the First World War Lithuania was occupied by tsarist Russia and Jacob attended a Russian primary school. Later he enrolled in a
gymnasium (secondary school) in the city of Siauliai. In 1919, at the age
of sixteen, the young Gens enlisted for service in the Lithuanian Army.
He was sent to study in an officers' school and graduated with the rank
of junior lieutenant.

Gens participated in the post-First World War Polish-Lithuanian
military confrontation, and was awarded a medal for his participation in
Lithuania's struggle for independence. After the war Gens completed
his secondary education in the city of Marjampole, and was promoted
to the rank of senior lieutenant. In 1924 Gens was transferred from

active duty into the reserves. He moved then to Ukmerge, a town in Eastern Lithuania, where he accepted a position at a Jewish school, teaching there Lithuanian language and physical education. In Ukmerge Gens became acquainted with, and married, Elvyra Budreikaite, a gentile Lithuanian woman employed in a local military detachment. Elvyra came from an intelligent Lithuanian family. She received her secondary education in Riga (Latvia), and was fluent in Lithuanian, Polish, Russian, German, and French.* In 1926 she bore a daughter, Ada, and in 1927 the family moved to Kaunas. In Kaunas Gens worked as an accountant in the Ministry of Justice, and studied, at the same time, at the Kaunas University. In 1935 he graduated from the university with a diploma in law and economics. In the late 1930's Gens was called back from the reserves, served for a while in the armed forces, and was promoted to the rank of captain.[5]

Gens had little contact with the Jewish community because most of his friends were military men. He belonged to the Lithuanian Nationalistic Union of Riflemen, and he was staunchly anti-Soviet. He had excellent relations with most Lithuanian army officers, and even under Nazi occupation they did not abandoned him. And yet, Gens never rejected his Jewishness. He was an earnest follower of he Revisionist brand of Zionism, lead by V. Zhabotinsky, and a member of *Brith-ha-hayal*, a paramilitary organization of the Zionists-Revisionists. He even once organized out of town a special camp to provide its members with military training. Gens combined thus his Lithuanian patriotism with a right wing Jewish nationalism. As a native of Lithuania, and a Jew, he believed that he had an obligation to serve both, the interests of his native country, as well as the national cause of the Jewish people. In both instances his main interest and contribution was mainly of a military nature. The Zionism of Gens was ideological rather than national, and he never intended to move to Palestine. He identified himself completely with the Lithuanian state.[6]

In the summer of 1940 when Lithuania was incorporated into the Soviet Union, Gens was the first to be fired from his job at "Lietukis," a state-private major Lithuanian enterprise. His personal employment card was taken away from him, and he was deprived thus of the right to live and work in Kaunas. He moved then in with his mother, and brother Solomon, in Vilnius where he was little known. At first his wife and daughter stayed for a while behind in Kaunas, but they soon joined him in Vilnius.

As a former officer in independent Lithuania Gens was persecuted by the Soviet regime and consequently was refused employment. He joined then the anti-communist underground and demonstrated once again his dedication to the Lithuanian national cause. With the help of an old comrade-in-arms, Colonel Usas, who was at that time the head of the health department in Vilnius, Gens managed to secure some temporary employment in the health department. Since he was paid by the hour he was not required to register with the personnel department and could remain out of sight. In June 1941 when most leading members of the local bourgeoisie, intelligentsia, and Lithuanian armed forces were exiled to Siberia, Gens was forced into hiding. Yet when the war started, on 22 June 1941, the notion of escape to the USSR, in order to avoid Nazi occupation, was rejected by Gens outright.

After the *Wehrmacht* entered Vilnius, in June 1941, Colonel Usas remained in charge of the city's health department. He then appointed Gens to the position of Director of the Jewish Hospital which until the creation of the ghetto in Vilnius was still under the jurisdiction of the city's health department.

Already in the first days of Nazi occupation, even before the ghetto in Vilnius was created, Gens was exposed to the humiliation and danger of being a Jew. One day the so-called "chapunes" or "catchers" invaded the apartment of the Gens family with the firm intention of arresting Gens. All those apprehended by the "catchers" were taken to Lukiszki prison, and from there transferred to Ponary for execution. Only the entreaties of Gens' wife, a Lithuanian woman, who literally kissed the hands of the murderer, saved Jacob Gens from unavoidable death. After having agreed to let Gens stay the "catcher" wanted to take away his brother who lived, with their mother, in the same apartment. The "catcher" could not apparently ignore the supplications of Elvyra Gens, and left the place empty handed.[7]

The Nazi occupation, and its racist laws, complicated Gens' family life and posed a grave danger particularly to his teenage daughter who was the product of a mixed marriage. According to one source, after the Germans entered Vilnius "Gens and his Lithuanian wife formally divorced in order to save her from sharing his fate, and his wife's sister took care of his daughter."⁸ According to another source, "when the ghetto was formed [Gens'] wife and daughter lived a short distance away under his wife's maiden name ... It was rumoured that the Gens couple had gone through a per forma divorce; that was not true ... Gens never denied the rumours."⁹

In the early days of the ghetto Gens continued in his job at the Jewish hospital. According to Ada Gensaite most members of the Judenrat in Vilnius, at that time, were respected members of the pre-war Jewish community in the city, but most of them were old, feared the Nazis, and did not have the slightest notion of how to deal with them. Anatole Fried, the first Judenrat chairman in the Vilnius ghetto, was acquainted with Gens and impressed by his work at the Jewish Hospital. He liked Gens' firmness, his self-assurance, and military bearing. The members of the Judenrat in the ghetto appreciated the way Gens managed the affairs of the hospital and repeatedly asked him to join the ghetto administration. In the end Gens succumbed to pressure and accepted the position of the ghetto police chief.¹⁰

Initially Gens' wife "opposed to his taking any conspicuous part in Jewish affairs .... yet he undertook being police chief only because, as he told his wife, 'I hope you understand that I cannot abandon the ghetto at a time when my people are suffering so much. I must stay and try do the best I can for the Jews of the ghetto'.... His wife says he never expected to act the role of God with power over human lives."¹¹ It is well known, however, that the road to hell is paved with good intentions. The role of Gens was even more entangled because he had to serve to different masters at the same time: the German bosses, as well as the helpless Jews for whose sake he undertook this task. It was clear from the outset that Gens embarked on an impossible mission, because the interests of the Jews in the ghetto, and those of the German rulers were totally irreconcilable. The main objective of the former was physical survival by any means, while the purpose of the latter was to murder as many Jews as soon as possible. Hence, by trying simultaneously to save as many Jews as possible, while keeping, at the same time, the hungry Nazi beast satisfied, Gens was forced to walk a tightrope.

Little by little, with the support of the German authorities, Gens usurped complete power in the ghetto, and in July 1942, the Judenrat was formally dissolved, and Gens was appointed as the "ghetto representative," or absolute ruler of the ghetto. In addition, the German authorities entrusted Gens with control over the Jewish councils in some ghettos in small towns in the Vilnius region, namely Oszmiana, Swieciany, Soly, and Michaliszki.

After the appointment of Gens as the head of the ghetto he made the following Announcement:

> "By Order of the *Gebietskommissar* of Vilna of July 12, 1942, I have assumed full responsibility for the ghetto as representative of the ghetto and Chief of Police.
> The basis of existence in the ghetto is work, discipline and order. Every resident of the ghetto who is capable of work is a pillar on which our existence rests.
> There is no room among us for those who hate work and in devious ways engage in crime.... I hereby proclaim a general amnesty, in this way permitting the criminals of yesterday to return to better ways....
> The order... does not apply to persons who committed.... murder; grievous or serious personal injury; insulting or physically attacking a policeman carrying out his official duties, or in connection with these duties; offenses against the authorities;...."[12]

As the chief of police, and later the head of the ghetto, Gens was granted by the Germans a number of privileges, of which ordinary ghetto Jews were usually deprived. He did not have to wear a yellow star of David patch on his chest and back, as all other Jews were required. Instead, he wore just a white and blue armband with the star of David, indicating his position as the head of the ghetto. He was free to leave the ghetto at any time he wished, and he could visit regularly his wife and daughter in the city. Moreover, his daughter who was half-Jewish, was not forced to move into the ghetto, as was the case with most other children from mixed marriages. Gens had also permission to carry a revolver and use a bicycle for transportation in the city. Both, Gens' mother and brother, Solomon, lived in the Vilnius ghetto. His brother was employed in the ghetto administration, and was in charge of the labour office in the ghetto. At another time he was assigned to responsible duties at the ghetto gate. Gens' other brother, Ephraim, was appointed in August 1941 to head the ghetto police in Siauliai, a city in North-Western Lithuania. He stayed in this initial position until March 1944.[13] Ephraim was the only brother of Gens to survive the Holocaust. From Siauliai he was transferred to the Dachau concentration camp in Germany where, at the end of the war, he was set free by the allied forces. When Ephraim returned after the war to Lithuania, to see whether any relatives survived the Holocaust, he was arrested by Soviet authorities and exiled to Vorkuta, in the Russian Far North. He was never permitted to return to Lithuania, and died in Moldova, a small Soviet republic in the southern regions of the USSR. A daughter of Ephraim Gens also survived the Holocaust and moved to Israel.[14]

As a former army officer Gens managed the ghetto administration and police with an iron grip, and he often behaved in a dictatorial manner, in particular with those who dared to question his decisions. He established rigid discipline and demanded loyalty and obedience from his subjects. In total more than 200 individuals were employed in the Jewish ghetto policing system. There were four police precincts in the ghetto, and a special precinct charged with the responsibility of guarding the ghetto gates. The gates were, of course, guarded at all times by Lithuanian policemen from the outside, but Jewish policemen were supposed to watch for the orderly passage of Jewish work brigades to, and from, work in the city. They were also required to make sure that Jews, returning from work to the ghetto, did not smuggle in any food or firewood. The Jewish ghetto gates guard, and its head, Levas, were known as a vicious bunch, but much of their violence was to impress the Germans and Lithuanians at the gate, and cover up for activities which benefited the ghetto. Some of the policemen at the gate supported the ghetto underground resistance movement, and assisted those who were smuggling arms into the ghetto.

The police had also a criminal division, an intelligence unit, as well as male and female civil agents. There was also a special group of so-called "snatchers." Their main objective was to uncover secret hiding places in the ghetto, and when required deliver workers to German enterprises. There were also several police "specialists" whose main task was to participate in the process of criminal investigation and with the help of physical force compel those detained to admit to their crimes and transgressions. Initially Jewish ghetto policemen carried sticks, but were otherwise unarmed. Occasionally when they were called upon to assist in speeding up Nazi deportation actions they were provided with guns.[15]

The issue of policing and ghetto administration is invariably complex, and the discussion of the roles of Judenrats and the Jewish ghetto police defies generalization. Some see Jewish policemen as Nazi collaborators, while others regard them as sorry victims. According to Adolf Eichmann "there can be no doubt that without the cooperation of the victims, it would hardly have been possible for a few thousand people, most of whom, moreover, worked in offices to liquidate many hundreds of thousands of other people...."[16] Eichmann fails, however, to note that in addition to the Germans, who were supervising the "Final Solution" from their offices, there were thousands of others, Germans and local Nazi collaborators, who have assisted the Nazis in their dirty work, and in many instances have actually been involved in the murder of innocent people.

The actions and motivation of each Jewish policeman, or member of the Judenrat in the Vilnius ghetto, merits separate judgement. Some Jewish policemen were drunk with power, they abused their Jewish subjects, and fulfilled the brutal orders of their German bosses with extraordinary zeal. Many such policemen were refugees from the western regions of Poland who came to Vilnius in September 1939. They had few friends or relatives in the city, and no ties with the local Jewish community. That made it easier for them to overstep the moral bounds that separated common decency from unacceptable behaviour. According to a highly generalized statement by Dina Porat "the Vilna ghetto police was despised by the public. It never functioned as if under compulsion by the Germans, but rather as if it wallowed in its illusory control over others."[17]

In the Lithuanian Central State Archive there is a list of forty-nine Jewish ghetto policemen who have allegedly participated in criminal activities against the Jewish ghetto population. Six of them were killed by the Germans. Seven were shot by Soviet partisans. Some others managed to avoid Soviet retribution by escaping in time to Poland. "The list was compiled on the basis of documentary materials and information obtained from comrade S. Garbelis, who was delegates to serve in the ghetto police by the underground [communist] party committee."[18] It is worthwhile to note, however, that since this list was produced by Soviet officials, already after the liberation of Vilnius from German occupation, it is possible to suspect that some bias was inherent in the process of producing the list. It is well known today that some of those executed by the pro-Soviet partisans were not implicated in any anti-Jewish criminal activity in the ghetto, but their murder was rather the result of internal political rivalries and disagreements. On the other hand, the Jewish policemen who were shot by the Nazis were killed not because they abused their Jewish subjects in the ghetto. Some, including Jacob Gens, were murdered simply because their services were no longer required, while others were uncovered in hiding places in the city, long after the ghetto was liquidated, and killed on the spot without delay.

These highly generalized accusations of the Jewish policemen notwithstanding, most policemen were decent young people appointed to positions they were forced to accept. They tried hard to maintain a balance between the need to serve a hated regime and provide a service to their downtrodden brethren. It was well known in the Vilnius ghetto that many Jewish policemen were active members of the underground resistance movement. By the summer of 1943, twelve F.P.O. members served in the ghetto police,[19] and many other ghetto policemen belonged to the Second Fighting Organization. These policemen informed the underground about possible Nazi actions; they assisted members of the underground in trouble with the ghetto administration, and, most importantly, they helped to bring in arms into the ghetto.

Officially, "the function of the Jewish police included: a) tasks carried out in response to German demands, b) functions limited to activities of the Judenrat ... in direct connection with German demands, and c) functions emanating from the internal need of the Jewish population."[20] As far as the Germans were concerned the most important task of the Jewish police was to uncover any illegal anti-Nazi activity developing within the ghetto. The Jewish police was also expected, from time to time, to assist the Germans in their deportation actions. In such cases, the ethical dilemma faced by each policeman was indeed immense. Each had to decide for himself whether he was to save his own skin by sacrificing the lives of his neighbours, friends, and relatives, or he was to protect his dignity by refusing to acquiesce to the demands of the Nazis. The choice was not an easy one, and often impulsive. German suspicion that a Jewish policeman tried to assist those targeted for deportation and murder was fraught with dangerous consequences, and it could imperil the life of the policeman in question, as well as his family.

The behaviour of each policeman was determined by his character traits, by the social environment which helped form his personality, as well as by the balance between good and evil in each individual. It was also influenced by the complex and personal relationship between the natural instinct of self-preservation and the moral principles inherited and acquired by each individual from his family, friends, and teachers. In the beginning, police service seemed to most conscripted young and inexperienced Jewish boys as a positive, valiant, and daring occupation. They did not realize yet then that some of them would be turned into passive tools of a manipulative murderous regime.

The Vilnius ghetto was created early in September 1941. Three weeks later, on 1-2 October 1941, the so-called "Yom Kippur" deportation action in the ghetto took place. German and Lithuanian units invaded then unexpectedly the ghetto and Gens feared that the snatching of people in the streets would end in a general massacre. He persuaded Schweinberger, the Gestapo officer in charge, to let the Jewish police do the job. That was when the Jewish police was called upon, for the first time, to assist the Nazis in rounding up ghetto residents. 2,200 individuals from the first ghetto were delivered by the Jewish police. They were taken to prison and later murdered in Ponary.[21]

Gens and the Jewish police participated also actively in the October-November 1941 so-called "yellow certificates" actions. "The Germans appreciated Gens's efforts, his erect, soldierly stance, his air of command. His prompt execution of orders put him on good terms with F. Murer [the German official in charge of Jewish affairs in the office of the *Gebietskommissar*] .... To the Germans he presented the image of a good and faithful servant."[22] That did not mean, of course, that Gens did not try, when possible, to save a Jewish life. During the "yellow certificates" action Gens stood at the ghetto gate and supervised the removal of Jews without certificates. On the surface, he was a willing and efficient tool of the German authorities in their savagery, yet when he could he did the opposite. According to the law a yellow certificate was issued to a worker, and it protected his or her family composed of no more than four people: the worker, his or her spouse, and no more than two children of under sixteen. At one point Gens managed, in the presence of SS officers, to save a boy from a family with three children by pushing the boy into the lap of a passing surprised father with only one child.[23]

Gens' involvement in assisting the Germans in their deportation actions was initially fostered by his desire to minimize the damage. Yet Gens abhorred the work he was forced to do. He wrote to his wife that "for the first time in my life I have taken upon myself to fulfil such task. My heart bleeds, but I shall always do whatever necessary for the Jews in the ghetto."[24] Gens was an inveterate optimist and he ardently believed that he will manage to save, at least some Vilnius Jews, from destruction, because the front and the Soviet Army were approaching, and the Germans will not have enough time to complete their atrocities. He once said: "We are forced to hide in places of concealment; we are driven to Ponary; we are left without families, but we have managed during these years [in the ghetto] to recreate our lives, to achieve more than the Aryans, because such is our nation - with a strong spirit and hope that it will survive."[25]

With the help of a combination of different means such as bribery, persuasion, submission, and duplicity Gens tried to sway Nazi decisions, slow the process of destruction, and improve the lot of the Jews in the ghetto. Thus, major Narusis, a former friend of Gens from the days in Kaunas, was presently employed by the Vilnius city administration and assigned the task of managing the living quarters in the area adjacent to the ghetto, most of which were vacant. Gens turned to Narusis and asked him to approach the German authorities and request permission to widen the boundaries of the ghetto. Indeed, Narusis obtained permission from the Germans to enlarge the living space of the ghetto, and the crowding inside the ghetto was somewhat eased.[26]

31 December 1941, Gens and a group of his colleagues assembled to celebrate the approaching New Year. Gens made a speech at this gathering, and he declared that despite the fact that he was forced, on numerous occasions, to stand at the ghetto gates during deportation actions, and witness how many Jews were led away to their death, he, and the Jewish police, fulfilled an important task. The same evening, the wife of Gens arrived in the ghetto. She was approached by several Jewish women who complained to her about the harsh deeds of her hus-

band. Gens' wife, however, tried to reassure the women that her husband was a decent man who performed an important task.[27]

It is asserted today by many that the assistance of Jewish ghetto officials, and the participation of the Jewish police, in German deportation actions hastened the liquidation of the ghettos and the destruction of East European Jewry. And it is suggested that in the case of Gens, in many instances "compliance turned into active collaboration with the murderers."[28] It is necessary, however, to point out that cooperation with the Nazi regime was never voluntary. It was rather the result of Nazi scheming and intimidation. In most cases the compliance with Nazi orders was forced upon the Jewish officials who were potential victims themselves. They were promised survival, but in return were forced to victimize those who were destined for immediate slaughter. In the end, after having been used and abused, most Jewish policemen and ghetto officials were murdered by the Nazis in cold blood.

It is erroneous to believe that without the help of Jewish policemen the Germans would fail to realize their savage plans. In fact, at the time of the so-called "great provocation," early in September 1941, before the ghetto in Vilnius was created, the Nazis killed in Ponary within several days close to 6,000 Jewish men, women, and children without the help of Jewish leaders or policemen. At that time, there was simply no Jewish police yet, and members of the Vilnius Judenrat were driven to their death together with the other Jewish victims. In the ghetto of Lwow, in Western Ukraine, Josef Parnes, the chairman of the local Judenrat, refused to hand over individuals for work camps, and consequently was murdered by the Nazis without much ado. After his death, the Jewish police in Lwow began snatching people to be sent to work camps.[29]

The Jews in the ghetto had a love-hate relationship with Gens. Those who lost relatives and friends in the deportation actions, supervised by Gens and the Jewish police, hated them and regarded Gens as a Nazi collaborator. Those, however, whom Gens' policies helped to survive slaughter, viewed him as their saviour. In general, in times of peace in the ghetto, the Jews both hated and respected Gens. They trusted him and doubted his sincerity, at the same time. They were happy to see, or imagine, that at least one Jew in the ghetto was shown some esteem by the Germans in charge, and was able to deal with the gentiles as an "equal." Most Jews in the ghetto were happy to delude themselves and often overestimated the potential of Gens to save the remaining Jews of Vilna . Gens' military bearing, his composure and self-confidence gave hope to the downtrodden Jews in the ghetto, but it also helped to deceive them and make them expect the impossible. Gens' boldness and aplomb were also partially to blame for his own personal failure and death. He obviously underestimated the duplicity of the Nazis who were ready to use the most savage means in order to reach their final goal.

1942 was the year of relative peace in the ghetto and Gens continuously fostered the idea of "life for work." The Jewish ghetto administrators were deceived by their German bosses into believing that the future of the ghetto was secure. The Jewish ghetto leaders, in turn, lulled the ghetto inhabitants into thinking that there was no danger to their existence. Gens was convinced that those Jews who were indispensable to the German war economy would survive. Hence, he advocated that the Jews must demonstrate to the Germans that they were extremely useful to them. They must give up easy and comfortable work places for more difficult ones, so as to be more useful to the German regime. According to Gens, that was necessary for the general welfare of the ghetto. "That is the corner-stone of our lives."[30]

In 1942, life in the ghetto, still in the shadows of the constantly lurking death, assumed up to a point a semblance of a normal life. Consequently, as in any normal social setting, incidents of crime, such as theft, robbery, and even murder, have become the subject of the day, and the new concern of the Jewish police. The ghetto had its own well organized justice system and court of law. Jews were sentenced by Jews for not carrying out German decrees, as well as for internal ghetto transgressions and crimes. Those arrested could be held in jail without trial for up to twenty-four hours. Court sentences usually varied from imprisonment for a few hours to up to six months, and fines up to 100.00 Reichsmarks. In the first half of 1942 there were 115 criminal trials in the Vilnius ghetto, involving 172 persons. During the same period 183 other persons were brought before individual magistrates and police judges. The appeal court in the ghetto was comprised of a full complement of five members of the judicial council. On one occasion it even authorized death sentences on ghetto Jews.[31]

Thus, early in 1942, a Jewish murderer in the ghetto was put on trial and convicted to six months of prison to be served in the ghetto jail on Lidska Street. Soon, however, he was removed from the ghetto by the Gestapo, and transferred to the Lukiszki prison in the city from where there was usually no return. In June 1942, two Jewish murderers in the ghetto were convicted by the ghetto court to death by hanging, and they were executed inside the ghetto. At the same time, a gang of forty children, involved in criminal activity, was uncovered by the police, and the operation of a bawdy house in the ghetto was thwarted by police agents. The police and the ghetto court also handled many cases of theft, physical abuse, speculation, and even family matters.

The position of Gens, as the head of the ghetto, exposed him to continuous attention and scrutiny from his ghetto subjects. And yet, Gens was not a superman, as some ghetto inhabitants imagined, but an ordinary human being with simple human needs and frailties. He was also a well educated and erudite man with many intellectual and cultural interests. A list of book, taken out by Gens from the ghetto library illustrates the breadth of his interests. It includes book by Jewish classics such as Sholom-Aleikhem, Apatoshu, and Zinger, as well as the four volume Jewish Encyclopaedia and the Jewish history by H. Graetz in Russian.[32]

His family affairs and personal life Gens kept private, but it was known in the ghetto that Gens visited regularly his wife and daughter in the city. They were also coming occasionally to the ghetto to visit Gens, and to attend performances of the ghetto theatre. Gens shared with his immediate family his ghetto problems, but avoided mentioning individual names. There was always a danger that his wife and daughter might be arrested and tortured, and he feared that under pressure they might be forced to reveal names.[33]

It seems also that despite his busy schedule, and constant pressure of his ghetto responsibilities, Gens had enough time to carry on, for a while, an intimate relationship with a another woman in the ghetto. Frances Penney, whose name in the ghetto was Franka Zilberman, was a young married woman from Warsaw. During her escape from the German invasion of Poland she parted with her unfaithful husband and turned up in Vilnius. At first she worked in the Gestapo, but after she lost her job there, Gens allegedly offered her a supervisory position in the ghetto workshops.

Franka-Frances Zilberman-Penney relates the following detail about her life in the Vilnius ghetto:

"the only bright side of my life was the pleasure of Gens' company. Whenever I would come to see him his place would become my refuge. Whenever he would come home burdened by a day of making harsh decisions, torn between his loyalty to his brethren and the bloody demands of the Germans that he as a Commandant of the ghetto was expected to carry out, I would try to disperse the heavy clouds hanging over his head. It would usually take a little time for him to relax, but eventually he would shake off his sadness and gloomy thoughts.... I, with his strong and protective arms around me, would delight in the atmosphere of tenderness and beauty. We were just a man and woman, giving each other what we both needed most - some fleeting moments of magical escape from the horror of reality."[34]

After Jacob Gens was executed, on 14 September 1943, Franka went with the brother of Gens to her lover's apartment. All they found there were two guns. "We have lost a compassionate leader," she exclaimed.[35]

1942 was the year when there were no major deportation actions in the Vilnius ghetto, and accordingly the reverence and respect granted to Gens, by the ghetto population, was at its highest level. Many Jews viewed him as their major benefactor, able to defend and protect them from all Nazi evils. That was, of course, another illusion. It did not take long before the short respite in ghetto life was shattered by unexpected events. In October 1942, the Nazis intended to kill 1,500 of the 2,300 Jews residing, at that time, in the ghetto of Oszmiana, some 50 km from Vilnius. Gens was summoned to the Gestapo, and was told to arrange for the surrender of those to be murdered. The local Judenrat in Oszmiana refused, however, to comply with the request. Gens haggled with the Germans and after a while managed to persuade them to reduce the number of victims requested to 400. On 23 October 1942, all the Jews of Oszmiana assembled in the marketplace, and 410 of them, mostly old and sick, were selected for destruction. Jewish ghetto policemen from Vilnius assisted the Lithuanian security forces which were actually involved in the act of killing.[36] "This ignominious deed shook Gens's prestige in the ghetto ... It showed how indifferent he was to life in the desire to save lives."[37]

The Oszmiana affair unsettled the relative tranquillity in the Vilnius ghetto and placed the relationship between Gens and his Jewish ghetto subjects in a new light. Gens tried hard to alleviate the situation, and convince the ghetto Jews of his good and sincere intentions. Four days after the Oszmiana massacre, on 27 October 1942, Gens called a meeting of the Jewish ghetto leadership and made a report about the recent events. Gens stated:

> "I asked you to come here today in order to relate to you one of the most terrible tragedies in the life of Jews - when Jews led Jews to their death. Once more I have to speak openly to you.
> A week ago Weiss of the SD came to us in the name of the SD with an order that we were to travel to Oszmiana. There were about 4,000 Jews in the Oszmiana ghetto and it was not possible to keep so many persons there. For that reason the ghetto would have to be made smaller - by picking out the people who did not suit the Germans, to take them away and shoot them.... When we received this order we replied: 'At your command.'
> Mr. Dessler and Jewish Police went to Oszmiana.... no fewer than 1,500 persons had to be taken away. We said that we could not provide such number. We started to bargain. When Mr. Dessler arrived with the report from Oszmiana, the number dropped to 800. When I went to Oszmiana with Weiss, the number dropped again to 600. In reality.... 406 old people were collected in Oszmiana. These old people were handed over.
> When Weiss came the first time and spoke about the women and children, I told him that old people should be taken. He answered: 'The old people would die off in any case during the winter and the ghetto has to be reduced in size now.'
> The Jewish police saved those who must live. Those who had little time left to live were taken away, and may the aged among the Jews forgive us. They were a sacrifice for our Jews and for our future.
> I don't want to talk about what our Jews from Vilna have gone through in Oszmiana. Today I only regret that there were no Jews [i.e. Jewish Police] when the *Aktion* was carried out in Kiemieliszki and Bystrzyca. Last week all the Jews were shot there, without any distinction. Today two Jews from Swieciany came to me and asked

me to save them....and today I ask myself what is to happen if we have once more to carry out a selection. It is my duty to tell them: my good Jews, away with you, it is not my wish to soil my hands and send my Police to do the dirty work. Today I will say that it is my duty to soil my hands, because terrible times have come over the Jewish people. If five million people have already gone it is our duty to save the strong and the young, not in years only, but in spirit, and not to indulge in sentimentality. When the Rabbi in Oszmiana was told that the number of persons required was not complete and that five elderly Jews were hiding in a *maline* (hiding place), he said that the *maline* should be opened. That is a man with a young and unshaken spirit.

I don't know whether everybody will understand this and defend it, and whether they will defend it after we have left the ghetto, but the attitude of our police is this - rescue what you can, do not consider your own good name or what you must live through.... From you, gentlemen, I want moral support. We all want to live to leave the ghetto. Today, as we work, it may be that not many of the Jews fully comprehend the danger in which we operate. None of us can know how many times every day he could get to Ponary....Today we must be strong. Those who have faith will say: The Almighty will aid us.

Those who have no faith must ask the aid of the spirit of Jewish patriotism and public feeling. To survive it all and to remain, after the ghetto, a human being fit for the great Jewish future....The Jewish people saw no blood in the whole of the 2,000 years. They saw fire, but blood they did not see. But now the ghetto has seen it. Jews have come from Ponary with bullets through their feet and hands....The Jewish people have become familiar with blood, and then one loses one's sentimentality."[38]

Some time later, when presenting prizes to two ghetto poets, Gens defended his actions in the following manner,

"I, Gens, lead you to your death; and I, Gens, want to save Jews from death. I, Gens, order hideouts to be blown up; and I, Gens, do all in my power to create work certificates, employment, and any-thing that serves the ghetto. *I calculate the amount of Jewish blood and not the price of Jewish honour.* If I am asked for 1,000 Jews I deliver them. For if we, Jews, do not deliver them, the Germans will come and take by force and then it will not be a question of 1,000 but of thousands and the entire ghetto will perish. By delivering hundreds I save thousands and by delivering 1,000 I save 10,000. You are the men of intellect and pen. You are not dealing with the filth of the ghetto. You will come out clean from the ghetto. And if you survive the ghetto you will say: 'we have come out with clean consciences.' But if I, Jacob Gens, survive, I shall come out soiled and with blood dripping from my hands. And yet I shall present myself willingly to be judged. To be judged by Jews. I will say: 'I did everything in my power to save as many Jews as possible from the ghetto and lead them to freedom. And in order that at least a remnant of Jews should survive, I personally had to lead Jews to their deaths; and so that some people should be able to leave the ghetto with clean consciences, I had to wallow in filth and act without conscience." [39]

Gens' response to the leaders of the religious community was in the same vein. When during the October 1941 deportation action in the ghetto, Rabbis sent a delegation to tell him that he was contravening Jewish law by making the choice who should live and who should die, Gens, who knew little, if anything, of Jewish law, responded that it was justifiable to surrender a part if the others would thereby be saved.[40]

Early in 1942, trying to secure the support of the creative intelligentsia in the ghetto, Gens readily agreed to a proposal made by communal leaders that the surviving Jewish intellectuals of Vilnius be put on the Judenrat's staff in order to provide them with some livelihood and relative security. Now, having learned about the Oszmiana affair, some of these intellectuals tried to justify Gens. Thus, referring to the action in Oszmiana, the venerable Yiddish scholar Zelik Kalmanovitsh noted in his diary, which survived the war,

"Praised be the God of Israel for sending us this man [Gens] .... The young people took upon themselves this difficult task. They put on the official caps with the shield-of-David emblems and went there and did what had to be done. Over 400 human beings perished; the old, the weak, the sick, and abnormal children. In this manner 1,500 women and children were saved. Had alien hands carried out that Aktion, 2,000 would have perished."[41]

Not all intellectuals, of course, agreed with Kalmanovitsh, but it was easy for those who owed Gens their lives to justify his actions.

Despite the complexity of daily life in the ghetto, and the constant danger to its existence, Gens provided the artistic community in the ghetto with continuous material and spiritual support. On 15 January 1943 the first anniversary of the establishment of the theatre in the ghetto was celebrated, and Gens addressed those marking this events. He said:

> "Last year they said that the theatre was just a fad of mine. 'Gens is amusing himself.' A year has passed and what do we see? It was not just a fad of Gens. It was a vital necessity. The little theatre, the first concert....after that - big performances followed - by the big schools in Vilna. For the first time in the history of Vilna we were able to get a curriculum of studies that was all Jewish. A big Writers' Association, big children's homes, a big day home, a wide Jewish life. Our care for children has reached a level never seen before in the Jewish life of Vilna. Our spiritual life reaches high, and we have already held a literary competition. A musical competition will be held in another few weeks.... How did the idea come up? Simply to give people the opportunity to escape from the reality of the ghetto for a few hours. This we achieved. These are dark and hard days. Our body is in the ghetto but our spirit has not been enslaved. Our body knows work and discipline today because this maintains the body. The spirit knows of tasks that are harder.
> Before the first concert they said that a concert must not be held in a graveyard. That is true, but the whole of life is now a graveyard. Heaven forbid that we should let our spirit collapse. We must be strong in spirit and in body.... I am convinced that the Jewish [life] that is developing here and the Jewish [faith] that burns in our hearts will be our reward. I am certain that the day of the phrase 'Why hast Thou deserted us?' will pass and we shall still live to see better days. I would like to hope that those days will come soon and in our time."[42]

In the months to come, as the ghetto underground resistance movement grew and became stronger, the relationship between Gens and the leaders of the underground became increasingly more important. From the outset Gens showed contradictory attitudes to the question of armed resistance in the ghetto, and his relationship with the F.P.O. was ambiguous at best. On the one hand, Gens showed some support to the resistance movement, while on the other, he wanted to muzzle and control it, because he feared that it could endanger the existence of the whole ghetto. On the one hand, "he assured a representative of the F.P.O. that at the appropriate time he himself would join them .... On the other hand, he fought against plans of escape to the forest and against storing arms in the ghetto."[43] Gens justified his position by fear of collective responsibility. At times, he kept aloof of what was going on in the ghetto underground and pretended to know nothing about its existence. Moreover, he knew about the production of weapons for the resistance movement in the ghetto workshops, but did nothing to interfere with it. Gens was on good terms with the communists in the F.P.O., clearly out of consideration for his own personal future after the expected Soviet victory. He had also open lines of communication with the Second Fighting Organization, and did nothing to thwart the activity of the resistance movement in the ghetto as long as it confined itself to propaganda and training.

The departure of young people from the ghetto to join the partisans in the forest was initially opposed by Gens for two reasons. First, if the escapees were apprehended by the Nazis ghetto residents could face collective punishment, and besides, Gens believed that only the presence of young people in the ghetto, able to work and produce for the Germans, could secure the continuous existence of the ghetto. In June 1943 Gens addressed this issue at a meeting of the ghetto police. He declared that

"... we are faced with the problem of escape to the forests. Here is my position: getting to the forest is easier for me than for any of you. Although I do not belong to the supporters of Bolshevism, being an ex-officer, a member of Brith ha-hayal and a policeman, I will be more willingly received than all of you, as I know how to use arms. But I don't want to go... because now there is the question: one or 20,000? ... Supposing 500 persons left. When I think of that, I put myself in Neugebauer's [Gestapo representative] place. If I were in his shoes, I would liquidate the whole Ghetto in one go, because one has to be an idiot to let the ghetto become a reserve force for partisans. But Neugebauer is no idiot. He is smarter than all of us... We can certainly say to ourselves that the forest is working for the benefit of the ghetto, working to bring liberation. Quite right. But my task is to protect the loyal ghetto so long as it exists. No one ought to be able to reproach me."[44]

Yet despite the ambiguous approach of Gens to the problem of resistance in the ghetto, his attitude to the underground should not be regarded as negative. He tolerated and assisted underground organizations. Sh. Brand, one of the leaders of the Second Fighting Organization, declared bluntly that "the first arms in our possession, I received from Gens, and the first hand gun in my hands was from Gens."[45] At another instance, Ch. Borowska, a leading member of the underground communist party organization in the ghetto, and a member of the F.P.O. command, declared that Gens gave her a gold coin for the purpose of procuring arms.[46] Occasionally, the Jewish police conducted searches in the ghetto and confiscated gold, jewellery, and other valuables. Gens used theses objects to bribe the Nazis, securing sometimes the release of Jews arrested by the Germans. He used also the same resources to reward those he saw fit in the ghetto, as well as to support causes he considered worthwhile, including underground resistance organizations.

No wonder the attitude of Gens to the underground resistance movement in the ghetto was ambivalent. His position was complicated and endangered by the sheer fact that the Germans knew that weapons were smuggled into the ghetto and suspected that Gens and the Jewish police did little to prevent it. On 15 May 1943 Gens addressed a meeting of brigadiers (leaders of labour units), supervisors and policemen. In his speech he specifically referred to a Jew who allegedly tried to buy a gun from a Pole. The Pole denounced the prospective buyer to the police and the Jew was arrested. Gens asserted:

"A few days ago I went to the Gestapo and spoke to the Commander of the SD there about the revolvers. I may tell you that he is not at all stupid. He said to me: 'From an economic point of view the ghetto is very valuable, but if you are going to take foolish risks and if there is any question of security, then I will wipe you out. And even if you get 30, 40, or 50 revolvers, you will not be able to

save yourselves and will only bring on your misfortune faster'.....
Today another Jew has been arrested for buying a revolver. I don't
yet know how this case will end. The last case ended fortunately
for the ghetto. But I can tell you that if it happens again we shall be
very severely punished. Perhaps they will take away those people
over 60, or children... Now consider whether that is worthwhile!!!
...As long as the ghetto remains a ghetto those of us who have the
responsibility will do everything we can so that nothing shall
happen to the ghetto. Nowadays a Jew's whole family is responsible
for him. [The person who tries to buy a gun in the city.] If that is not
enough, then I will make the whole room responsible for him, and
if even that is not enough - the apartment and even the building."[47]

The above notwithstanding, and despite the misgivings of Gens
about the departure of young people from the ghetto, Gens did not
forcibly prevent the flight of young Jews from the ghetto to the forest,
nor did he surrender to the Germans any of those who intended to
escape. According to A. Tory, "when people started to flee to the forest
in an organized fashion Gens helped them. He let them leave the ghetto
through his own private alleyway. He always kept the key to it in his
pocket."[48] All the same, in the summer of 1943, the relationship between Gens and the F.P.O. became extremely tense, if not completely
antagonistic. On the one hand, Gens was looked upon by the F.P.O.
leaders as a helpless pawn in the hands of the Germans, while on the
other, the members of the underground in the ghetto obviously overestimated his potential in dealing with the Germans, and they hoped, without good reason, that he could protect the ghetto from deportations
and liquidation. Gens resented the fact that the underground leaders
ignored his rule and were ready to challenge his decisions, if necessary,
even by force.

The first test of strength between Gens and the F.P.O. took place
on 26 June 1943. Joseph Glazman, a former Zionist-Revisionist leader
in Lithuania, and the editor of the Revisionist newspaper *Hamdina,* was
born in the Lithuanian town of Alytus, and moved to Vilnius after the
city was transferred to Lithuanian rule. In the ghetto he served in the
capacity of deputy chief of the Jewish ghetto police. At the same time
he was a member of the F.P.O. command staff. At one point, after he
contradicted the ghetto administration policies, and challenged the ab-

solute power of Gens, he resigned from the ghetto police. He was then reappointed to another position in the ghetto administration and delegated to the town of Swieciany, some eighty kilometres from Vilnius, to assist the local ghetto administration. Glazman refused to move, and accused the police and ghetto authorities of collaborating with the enemy. In reply,

> "Gens had ordered the arrest of Joseph Glazman, ... one of the most popular figures in the Vilnius ghetto. Arrested by the Jewish police, Glazman ..., was being taken to a labour camp. Suddenly an armed FPO unit materialized near the ghetto gate, stopped the police ..., and freed Glazman .... Gens did not dare to punish the FPO. Instead, he negotiated with them, asking them to help save his prestige in the ghetto by having Glazman report voluntarily to the labour camp for one week. To avoid further confrontation, the F.P.O. agreed, after having received assurances about Glazman's safety."[49]

The confrontation between Gens and the F.P.O., and the power struggle between them, reached its highest level during the Witenberg affair. The F.P.O. vacillated at first and refused to abandon its leader to fate. Under pressure it relented and was forced to surrender Witenberg without a fight. Gens had his mind made up from the outset. He was all along for the surrender of Witenberg to the German authorities. Today, some question the determination of Gens not to challenge his German bosses, and accuse him of capitulating to the Nazis. Thus, for example, Eric Sterling asserts:

> "I believe that Gens made the wrong choices when he advocated passive compliance and when he turned over Wittenberg to the Gestapo, because he must have known that the Nazis planned to liquidate the ghetto shortly thereafter, as part of the Final Solution, and armed resistance was the only hope for the 20,000 Jews who had thus far escaped death .... [In an uprising] perhaps some Jews would die while many thousands more would escape .... the forest ... lay approximately four miles away."[50]

It is obvious to any informed survivor of the Vilnius ghetto, or diligent student of its history, that Sterling's conclusions are too optimistic, if not totally wrong. Drawing on the Warsaw ghetto experience it was clear, at that time, to any resident of the Vilnius ghetto, that most Jews would perish in an anti-Nazi revolt, and that only the few lucky ones would manage to escape. Most Jews in the ghetto were unarmed and knew nothing of the partisans. Moreover, few had hiding places prepared in advance in the city. In addition, the forest, that Sterling refers to, might indeed have been located several miles from the city, but the whole region in the vicinity of Vilnius was controlled by Germans, their local Lithuanian collaborators, or the Polish A.K. The Soviet partisans instead, the only ones ready to accommodate some of the escaping ghetto Jews, were much farther from the city, and not less than some thirty miles away. In fact, not Gens but rather Witenberg's communist associates and the F.P.O. leaders convinced Witenberg that his surrender was inevitable. Gens orchestrated the anti-Witenberg mood in the ghetto, he was playing on the fears of the people, but without the assistance of the F.P.O. there was no way the Jewish police could have apprehended Witenberg.

In the summer of 1943 increasing underground activity, connected with the contemplated departure of young people from the ghetto to the forest, was fostered by the arrival from the countryside of young Jewish guides who were prepared to lead ghetto youths into the region controlled by Soviet partisans in Western Belorussia. One of them was M. Shutan, a native of Swieciany. He had established contacts with Soviet partisan leaders in Western Belorussia and was ready to lead Jewish fighters into the forest. He appeared in the ghetto on several occasions. He was in touch with the F.P.O., as well as with other smaller independent youth groups. On one occasion Shutan was arrested by the Jewish police and brought to see Gens. After an interview, Gens set Shutan free and permitted him to lead a group of young people from the ghetto to the forest. At their meeting, on 12 June 1943, Gens told Shutan: "I know of the existence of the F.P.O., and all its arms caches. I know a time will come that I will need them .... When the time for the destruction of the ghetto comes, we shall need all the armed boys. We'll all fight then."[51]

After the Witenberg affair, Shutan appeared in the ghetto again. He came on behalf of Colonel F. Markov, a commander of a partisan brigade in Western Belorussia. Shutan approached the F.P.O. leaders, suggesting that the time was ripe to leave the ghetto and join the partisans in the forest. The F.P.O. leadership was not ready to move yet, and refused Shutan's offer to lead them into the forest. Then Shutan went to see Gens. When he arrived at Gens' office the latter was already informed about Shutan's presence in the ghetto, as well as of his meeting with the F.P.O. command.

According to Shutan, his discussion with Gens was straightforward and candid. Gens said that he did not deceive Witenberg, but he could not sacrifice the existence of the ghetto for the latter's safety. Gens expected the F.P.O. to fight for its leader. Instead, he claimed, his communist friends had abandoned and betrayed him in his time of need. Gens spoke of the F.P.O. leadership with derision. Their handling of the Witenberg affair undermined his faith in the combat readiness of this organization. Gens asserted that he knew all along that

> "they were cowards ... writers, poets, dreamers ... who imagined themselves to be ... the main power and spirit in the ghetto. They wanted to advise, dictate, and rule." Gens claimed that Glazman "wanted to give him [Gens] orders." Gens suggested that if that was the case "Glazman should have become the head of the ghetto administration and enforce any policy he desired." That would require, however, dealing directly with the Gestapo which Glazman obviously did not relish. Glazman "preferred that Gens would negotiate with the Gestapo, so that he could act and give orders from behind his back." [52]

Gens stated that he knew that the partisans were ready to accept into their ranks only those who were young, able-bodied, and armed, while his responsibility was to protect and try to save all those who had no means of arming themselves, or possibility of escape.

In the summer of 1943 Gens was under tremendous pressure from different directions, and one might question some of his decisions, but his motives were always sincere. Thus, for example, on 12 June 1943 a Jewish guard at the ghetto gate stopped a Jewish man who brought a hidden gun into the ghetto. The armed young Jew killed the Jewish policeman who searched him, and wanted to take away the gun. Gens, who was called immediately to the gate, arrived and shot, in turn, to death the young smuggler. The policeman, Moshe Gingold, was a refugee from Warsaw, while Chaim Levin, the armed young man, was a former

Jewish policeman in the Swieciany ghetto. This incident clearly corroborates the hideous nature of Nazi rule which created a system in which one victim was forced to exploit, abuse, or even murder, another one. Both young men killed, as well as Gens, were victims of the tragic times. The Jewish Vilnius ghetto policeman fell at his post, in the process of fulfilling his complicated duties. The man from Swieciany fell protecting his dignity and his right to have a gun which could help him fight the oppressor, and resist indiscriminate slaughter . Gens acted, perhaps, hastily and instinctively, but he was, in a sense, a victim as well. He was abused by his Nazi bosses and forced daily to demonstrate his reliability and trustworthiness. Moreover, Gens killed the armed Jew so the Germans could not arrest, torture, and interrogate him about the source of his weapon.[53]

Gens who acted as a self-righteous dictator, and who until the very last moment believed in himself and his mission, was a controversial figure. Similarly, the post-war assessment of his activity is controversial and contradictory. Some call him a martyr for the Jewish people, while others saw in his end justified retribution for his villainies. According to Reuben Ainsztein

> "no other ghetto leader went so far in serving the Nazis as Gens ....
> Nor did any other ghetto leader play such an effective part in sabotaging Jewish participation in the partisan movement .... His inner moral corruption [rather] than the urge of self-preservation and the attractions of an easy life ... dictated his behaviour .... [and] he found it possible to believe that he had a mission to fulfil and that he knew what was good for his Jewish subjects."[54]

Leonard Tushnet assessed Gens' personality differently. To him

> " Gens was a man of noble ideals, of a free and independent Lithuania, ideals of a Palestine conquered by the Jews to be their natural homeland. He saw no contradiction between the two. While the Jews were in the diaspora they should be strong supporters of the nations that shelter them, not separatists demanding special privileges nor cosmopolitans denying patriotic bonds .... Gens was a very special practical idealist, willing to make immediate compromises in the interests of a future goal. Without illusions about the

German hatred of the Jews he, nevertheless, clung to the illusion that he could minimize the results of that hatred .... Gens set the moral tone for the ghetto and made it a place where no one informed on pregnant women, or doctors treating contagious diseases, or on official and unofficial smuggling .... He was incorruptible and the example of incorruptibility was ever present before the police. There were neither bribe takers nor influence peddlers .... In the end he realized he had been only a tool, that he had succeeded in nothing but facilitating the extermination of the very Jews he wanted to save.[55]

Indeed, for all his weaknesses and wrongdoing Gens was not a traitor, nor a conscious collaborator with the Nazis. He did not share with them any common goals and aspirations. Collaborators supported the Nazi regime out of ideological conviction, or out of a desire to gain power and riches. That was not the case with Gens. He might have assisted the Germans, but that was not his aim. He never doubted that the Germans will lose the war. As many other Jewish leaders under Nazi occupation Gens was coerced by Nazi terror to submit and comply. He tried to protect his Jewish subjects to the best of his limited possibilities, believing that by surrendering the weak and the old to the thirsty-for-blood Nazi extermination machine he was buying time and saving the young and able-bodied. The ghetto Jews, however, expected from him more than he could deliver.

On 13 September 1943, Martin Weiss, a Gestapo officer who had no use for Jews, but who liked Gens, warned him that he was on the list of those to be executed. He advised him to disappear. Gens replied "No, if I, the chief of the ghetto, run away, thousands of Jews will pay with their lives for my desertion."[56]

The following day, on 14 September 1943, Gens and Desler were summoned to the Gestapo headquarters by its chief *Obersturmfuhrer* Rolf Neugebauer, who was in charge of the Gestapo in Vilnius from February 1942 to October 1943. According to one source, Desler was sent back to the ghetto, while Gens was put in a small jail cell. At 6.00 P.M. he was shot by the chief of Gestapo. According to another source "Neugebauer told Gens that the ghetto was about to be liquidated and, therefore, he was no longer needed. But he added that since Gens had fulfilled his role faithfully, he would have the honor of being shot by the

Gestapo leader himself. And with these words, he shot him.... It was also said in the ghetto that Dessler informed on Gens, saying that he had helped the Underground. In any case, Dessler knew in advance what was going to happen but did not tell Gens."[57] Rumours circulated in the ghetto all along that S. Desler was a Gestapo agent who sought to uncover any underground activity in the ghetto. He was in contact with, and reported to, Meyer, who was in charge of Jewish affairs at the German Security Police and the SD, and Martin Weiss, the head of the German special security squad.[58]

The Germans used and abused Gens and killed him when his services were no longer needed, just a week before the final liquidation of the ghetto in Vilnius. Gens could have, perhaps, saved himself. After all he was a former captain in the Lithuanian Army, his wife was not Jewish, and he had many useful contacts in the local Lithuanian community. But it was below his dignity to try escape danger and cowardly to abandon those from whom he constantly demanded trust.

The wife of Gens and her daughter, Ada, lived, at that time, on Geliu (Kwiatowa) Street, within walking distance from the ghetto. Soon they found out about the execution of their husband and father. M. Smilgowski, a Jewish ghetto policeman , arrived and informed them that the Gestapo was looking for them and suggested that they should disappear from site as soon as possible. Within minutes Mrs. Gens, and her daughter Ada, left their apartment on Geliu Street and went into hiding. The first night they spent in the apartment of the Righteous Gentile, Ona Simaite. A Lithuanian woman, Simaite worked as a librarian at the Vilnius University. She saved many Jewish children, as well as many precious documents and publications from the YIVO and Strashun libraries. Later Mrs. Gens and her daughter moved into the Lithuanian countryside where they were hiding until the end of the Nazi occupation. After liberation Mrs. Gens and her daughter lived for a while in Soviet Lithuania. In 1945 they left for Poland, and later settled in Australia. In 1953 they moved to the USA.[59]

The news about the execution of Gens raised the tension in the ghetto. According to Chaim Lazar,

"everyone saw this as a sign that the remaining Jews were about to be exterminated .... The Jews grieved over the tragedy of Gens. One could   say he was wrong, but everyone knew that he was not a traitor. Whatever he did as head of the ghetto, he did for his people. His methods were wrong and one cannot find any justification for turning Jews over to the Gestapo under any conditions. But he did not sell himself to the Gestapo. He truly and naively believed that he could deceive them, and   that through a policy of concessions and postponements he could keep at least a small number of Jews alive."[60]

Gens was one of the major tragic figures of the ghetto in Vilnius. Basically an upright man, of dignified bearing, he believed in justice and common decency. Life forced him to serve a base cause, but till the last moment he believed that his activity will   yield positive results. His straightforward and truthful military approach to life, however, was no match to the perfidious nature of Nazi politics and diplomacy. He failed not for lack of faith or dedication, but because his cause was doomed from the outset. No individual was permitted to slow the operation of the Nazi extermination machine, and interfere with the course of the "Final Solution."

Conclusion

VILNIUS, THE CURRENT CAPITAL OF INDE-
pendent Lithuania, is close to 700 years old. Over the years, the rulers
of the city changed many times, and so did the name of the city. The
population of the city grew steadily and before the beginning of the
First World War it was just under 250.000. Today it is close to 600.000. A
firm Jewish presence in the city has been established soon after its foun-
dation. Since the seventeenth century Vilnius has been known as the
Jerusalem of Lithuania.

The evolution of Jewish life in Vilnius progressed gradually, and it
was largely conditioned by the political situation in the country and the
generosity of its rulers. The number of Jews in the city fluctuated, but at
different times, close to half of all city inhabitants were Jewish. By the
middle of the nineteenth century, Vilnius was one of the main centres
of Yiddish and Hebrew secular and religious learning, as well as of Jewish social, cultural, and political activity in the diaspora.

The capture of Vilnius by the *Wehrmacht*, in June 1941, changed
the face of the city forever. Under Nazi rule the Jews of Vilnius were
exposed to the most heinous crimes of torture and murder. At first,
thousand of innocent Jews were executed, en masse, in the Paneriai
(Ponary) forest, on the outskirts of the city. Later, those who survived
the initial massacre were confined within the walls of a ghetto, and forced
to work in support of the Nazi war machine. Most ghetto Jews worked

hard and deluded themselves that their service to the German war economy would save their lives. Few, however, trusted the sincerity of the Nazis, and gave no credence to their promises.

The ghetto in Vilnius operated as an ostensible mini-state. It had its own internal Jewish administration, including a Jewish ghetto police, a court, and a jail. The ghetto system of government was a devilish invention of the Nazis. It was created with the purpose of deceiving the Jews. By providing those herded together within the ghetto walls with meagre means of physical survival, and a false sense of security, the Nazis were able to perpetrate and facilitate their next act of mass murder. Conditions of life in the ghetto were intense and extremely difficult. Cultural, social, and intellectual life alleviated, in some measure, the pervading doom and pessimism, and served as an expression of spiritual resistance, and an escape from the indignities of daily life, but there was no security anywhere, and death lurked from behind each corner.

The above notwithstanding, there were many young people in the Vilnius ghetto who refused to accept the inevitable, and submit to the Nazis without a fight. From the early days of Nazi occupation, politically conscious Jews began to gather, organize, procure weapons, and get ready for an armed confrontation with the Nazi enemy. Early in 1942 was established the so-called F.P.O., or the United Partisan Organization. Somewhat later was founded the so-called Second Fighting Organization. The main objective of these organizations was to procure arms and prepare for the forthcoming battle with the Germans and their local collaborators. The strategies and battle plans of the two organizations, however, were totally different. The first objective of the F.P.O. was to protect the dignity of the ghetto Jews by fighting the Nazis inside the ghetto when the time for the final liquidation of the ghetto would come. The leaders of the Second Fighting Organization, instead, believed that fighting the Nazis within the walls of the ghetto was a futile endeavour, and advocated a speedy departure of all able-bodied young Jews to the forest, with the purpose of joining there the pro-Soviet partisan brigades. There were also in the ghetto many small unaffiliated armed groups of youngsters who tried to escape from the ghetto into the nearby forests.

In the summer of 1943 the Vilnius ghetto had one of the best organized underground resistance movements in the Nazi occupied territories, and the Jewish fighters represented a considerable force. And yet, the ghetto was liquidated in September 1943 without any significant Jewish opposition to the Nazis. The political and ideological disagreements, and continuous squabbling between different underground groups on issues of resistance strategy in the Vilnius ghetto, hampered the underground activity of the resistance organizations in the ghetto, and precluded the participation of many unaffiliated youths in the battle with the oppressor. Moreover, the entangled relationship between the ghetto Jewish administration and the leaders of the resistance movements in the ghetto complicated the situation further, hastening even, in all probability, the liquidation of the ghetto.

In ordinary circumstances the plurality of opinions and the dialectic process of logical inquiry can lead to a synthesis of different points of view, and a course of action in which the interests of the majority, and the simple masses, become the practical guide for action. In ghetto conditions, however, when the span between physical survival and destruction, between life and death, was minimal, no thorough process of democratic consultation was possible, and ghetto leaders were often forced to adopt decisions instinctively, basing them on false political, ideological, and even personal premises.

The three tragic heroes discussed in the book played a crucial role in the history of the Vilnius ghetto. Yitzhak Witenberg was the leader of the F.P.O., and the main proponent of the idea that the underground resistance fighters had a moral responsibility to stay in the ghetto and, in time of need, defend its Jewish inhabitants. According to Witenberg, early departure to the forest was tantamount to desertion and cowardice. Yechiel (Ilya) Sheinbaum, the leader of the Second Fighting Organization, disagreed with this strategy and argued that it was a futile act of self-deception. He insisted that fighting the Nazis inside the ghetto would do little to help the majority of the ghetto Jews. Moreover, he claimed, it would endanger the lives of the ghetto resistance fighters who, as members of partisan detachment in the forest, could make a distinct contribution to the general anti-Nazi war effort.

Jacob Gens was at first the head of the Ghetto Jewish police, and later, since the summer of 1942, the head, or representative of the ghetto. He was charged with the duty of maintaining law and order in

the ghetto, assisting, at the same time unwittingly, the German administration in its sinister plans of murder and destruction. Gens tried,
however, to do everything within his limited possibilities to minimize
the damage and save as many Jewish lives as possible.

Yitzhak Witenberg, Yechiel (Ilya) Sheinbaum, and Jacob Gens come
from different backgrounds. Prior to 1939, and particularly before the
German invasion of the USSR, they belonged to different antagonistic
social and political groups which were in constant political combat with
each other. Each of the three had a different vision of the future, but all
faced the same destiny.

Witenberg was a communist and labour leader in Wilno and a Jewish internationalist. Many Jewish communists, before the war, have for-
saken their Jewish spiritual roots and sought salvation in the creation of
a new classless internationalist society in which there would be no distinction between different ethnic and national groups. Sheinbaum was a
Zionist, from the eastern regions of Poland, who identified with the
Jewish historical past and believed that the survival of the Jewish people
as a nation was inherently connected with their return to the Jewish
ancestral home in Israel. Gens was an assimilated Lithuanian Jew, with
Zionist-Revisionist connections, and married to a gentile woman.

The tragedies of the three individuals discussed in the book could
be examined within the general perimeters of the notion "tragedy," which
has evolved over the centuries. The term "tragedy" in literature and
drama was initially defined by the Greek philosopher Aristotle (d. 322
BC), it implied the imitation of an action in drama that was serious,
complete in itself, and of a certain magnitude. Such action was supposed
to rouse pity and fear in the spectators, and then purge them of these
emotions. The tragic hero, a man neither villainous nor exceptionally
virtuous, moved from happiness to misery through frailty or some error
of judgement. He moved us to pity, because his misfortune was greater
than he deserved, and to fear because we recognized similar possibilities
and consequences in our own fallible selves.

In the Middle Ages tragedy was in most instances conceived to be
simply the story of an eminent person who, deservedly or undeservedly,
was brought from prosperity to wretchedness by an unpredictable turn
of fate. Moreover, the tragic hero did not have to be a man with a tragic
flaw. It could be one who turned great gifts to evil purposes and de-

served his destruction. In Modern Drama the downfall of the tragic hero is often caused by the evil of society rather than by fate or a character flaw within oneself.

The distinction between the popular and the literary meaning of "tragic hero" is not merely academic. In real life some tragic heroes may reach out for new spiritual heights only to face destruction without having achieved anything positive. Others may selflessly seek compromises in circumstances when nothing positive is possible. In both instances, however, the move towards inevitable fate may provide us with new meaning, and a hint at the complexity of human nature and the human condition.

The tragedies of Witenberg, Sheinbaum, and Gens contain elements of classical Greek, as well as of modern drama. The actions of the three are serious, but they turn out disastrously for the characters discussed. The tragedies arouse pity and fear, but they hardly purge the reader from his or her emotions. Just as it is often the case in modern drama, the downfall and death of the characters discussed here is caused by the evil of society rather than by personal shortcomings or faulty character traits.

Witenberg, Sheinbaum, and Gens were victims of social and political evil instigated by the murderous German Nazi regime. But not only. They were also victims of a number of intricate circumstances which made their survival difficult, if not totally impossible. Witenberg was betrayed by a communist colleague who was tortured by his Nazi jailors, and divulged the former's complicity in the anti-Nazi underground in the city. Later, Witenberg was abandoned to fate and persuaded to surrender by his communist comrades, and colleagues from the F.P.O. command staff, the organization he headed.

Sheinbaum was the only one, of the three, to fall in open battle with the Nazi enemy within the ghetto. He was also the most prominent ghetto underground leader who consistently opposed fighting the Germans inside the ghetto. Sheinbaum did not pretend that his objective was to save the lives, or the honour, of the ghetto masses. He advocated, instead, the escape of those under his command into the forest, in order to avoid the daily dangers of ghetto life, and when necessary face the enemy in more favourable conditions. In time of adversity, however, Sheinbaum did not shun responsibility. When he was sent by his colleagues, the leaders of the F.P.O., an organization he allegedly joined in good faith, to defend a defenceless position, he was ready to partake in battle, and he was exposed to extreme danger. Indeed, he was the first to offer armed resistance to the Germans in the ghetto, yet at the time of battle the military support he was promised never materialized.

Gens was duped by his German bosses. He served them diligently, and they, in turn, assured him, time and again, that the future of the ghetto was secure, and his personal safety guaranteed. But when his role was finished, they killed him without much ado. Of the three, Gens was the one who perhaps had the best chance to survive. He accepted, however, the challenge and instead of trying to save his own skin by hiding went to face his killers. His proud nature could not accept personal failure and he preferred to face destiny rather than try to escape.

The main objective of all three, Witenberg, Sheinbaum, and Gens, was Jewish personal and communal survival. All three resisted the Nazi intentions. Initially, they refused to accept the Nazi verdict that all Jews were to be indiscriminately slaughtered. Later, each of them resisted the Nazi designs in his own peculiar way. Witenberg and Sheinbaum joined the underground resistance movement in the ghetto and were ready to face the enemy with arms in hand. Gens resisted the Nazis in a different way. He haggled, cajoled, prevaricated, and bribed the Germans, trying to buy time. He sincerely believed that his actions will minimize the damage, slow the process of deportation and murder, and make possible the survival of the remaining Jews in the Vilnius ghetto.

The deaths of all three contain elements of suicide. Witenberg knew that there was no way back from the Nazi prison, and, indeed, there are indications that he committed suicide in jail before the Gestapo could interrogate and torture him. Sheinbaum's challenge to the Nazis in the ghetto was a deed generated by instinctive emotions of anger, hate, and a desire of revenge, but it was also a suicidal act replete with extreme danger. There was no way to overcome the overwhelming forces of the enemy, and little likelihood of survival in direct armed confrontation with the SS. The death of Gens was a conscious act of self-destruction, because he was warned by others that his murder was imminent. His surrender to fate was, in a sense, an admission of failure and his final escape from a world full of evil. It was a statement to the effect that the Germans deceived him, and that his efforts to save the remnants of the

Vilnius Jewish community were futile.

Witenberg, Sheinbaum, and Gens perished fighting the pernicious plans of the oppressor, and their tragic deaths contain elements of courage, dedication, and determination. Each of them acted in a manner his conscience prescribed, yet in the end their deaths might appear futile. However, that was not the way they saw it, because each of them sacrificed his life for a cause and an idea.

Endnotes

CHAPTER ONE

[1] Howard M. Sachar, *Modern Jewish History* (New York 1963), 29.

[2] Ibid., 69.

[3] Arunas Bubnys, "Special SD and German Security Police Squads in Vilnius (1941-1944)," in *The Days of Memory*, ed. by E. Zingeris (Vilnius 1995), 182.

[4] Israel Cohen, *Vilna* (Philadelphia 1992), 4.

[5] Ibid., 30.

[6] G. Agranovskii and I. Guzenberg, *Litovskii Ierusalim* (Vilnius 1992), 49.

[7] Yitzhak Arad, Yisrael Gutman, and Abraham Margaliot, eds., *Documents on the Holocaust* (Jerusalem 1981), 378-82, also in E. Rozauskas, ed., *Documents Accuse* (Vilnius 1970), 131-58.

[8] Ibid., 383.

[9] Yitzhak Arad, *Ghetto in Flames* (Jerusalem 1980), 49-50.

[10] Bubnys, 183.

[11] Arunas Bubnys, *Vokieciu okupuota Lietuva. 1941-1944* (Vilnius 1998), 271.

[12] Ibid., 185.

[13] See: "The Jaeger Report" in E. Klee, W. Dressen, V. Ries, *The Good Old Days* (New York 1988), 46-58.

[14] *Encyclopaedia Judaica, vol. 16 (Jerusalem 1971), 148.*

[15] Lietuvos Centrinis Valstibines Archivas - Lithuanian Central State Archive (In future quotes referred to as L.C.V.A.), F. R643, Ap. 3, B. 4152, L. 11.

[16] Irina Guzenberg, "The Vilnius Ghetto and the Population Census of 1942,". *The Jewish Museum. Vilnius Ghetto: Lists of Prisoners*, vol. 1 (Vilnius 1996), 55.

[17] L.C.V.A., F. R643, Ap. 3, B. 4152, L. 321.

[18] Leonard Tushnet, *The Pavement to Hell* (New York 1972), 172.

[19] R. Margolis, "Pogrindine antifasistine organizacija FPO Vilniaus gete (1942-1943)," in the *Days of Memory*, 298.

[20] L.C.V.A., F. R1421, Ap. 1, B. 4, L. 2.

[21] Arad, Gutman, and Margaliot, 394-5.

[22] Solon Beinfeld, "Health Care in the Vilna Ghetto," *Holocaust and Genocide Studies*, vol 12, no. 1, Spring 1998, 66-98.

[23] L.C.V.A., F. R1421, Ap. 1, B. 4, L. 2.

[24] L.C.V.A., F. R643, Ap. 3, B. 30, L. 2.

[25] Joshua Sobol, "The Passion of Life in the Ghetto," in *The Days of Memory* (Vilnius 1995), 247-9.

[26] Herman Kruk, *Togbuch fun vilner geto* (New York 1961), 359.

[27] Ibid., 136.

[28] *The Days of Memory*, 248.

[29] Sobol., 250.

[30] A. Sutskever, *Fun Vilner geto* (Moscow 1946), 114-21.

[31] Sachar, 445.

[32] Arad, Gutman, Margaliot, 456-7.

[33] Yisrael Gutman and Cynthia J. Haft, eds., *Patterns of Jewish Leadership in Nazi Europe. Proceedings of the Third Yad Vashem International Historical Conference, Jerusalem, April 4-7, 1977* (Jerusalem 1979), 188-9.

[34] Arad, 420.

[35] L.C.V.A., F. R1399, Ap. 1, B. 33, L. 4.

[36] Bubnys, "Special SD and German Security Police...",186-7.

CHAPTER TWO

[1] A. Sutskever, *Fun Vilner geto* (Moscow 1946), 191.

[2] Evsey Tseitlin, ed., *Jewish Museum. Vilnius Ghetto: Lists of Prisoners, vol. 1* (Vilnius 1996), 327. According to another source the name of Witenberg's wife was Etel. See endnote No. 33.

[3] Mark Dworzecki, *Yerushalaim de-Lita in kamf un umkum* (Paris 1948), 380.

[4] Yisrael Gutman and Livia Rothkirchen, eds., *The Catastrophe of European Jewry* (Jerusalem 1976), 373-4.

[5] Dworzecki, 343.

[6] Yitzhak Arad, Yisrael Gutman, and Abraham Margaliot, eds. *Documents on the Holocaust* (Jerusalem 1981), 433.

[7] Yehuda Bauer and Nathan Rotenstreich, eds., *The Holocaust as Historical Experience* (New York 1981), 252.

[8] Yitzhak Arad, *Ghetto in Flames* (Jerusalem 1980), 229.

[9] Reuben Ainsztein, *Jewish Resistance in Nazi-Occupied Eastern Europe* (London 1974), 491.

[10] Some of the information about the internal F.P.O. politics are provided by N. Reznik, one of the F.P.O. organizers, and later command staff member of the organization in an unpublished type script, distributed by Reznik among his friends, and in possession of the author of this book. See: N. Reznik, "Geshikhte fun F.P.O." For the history of the F.P.O. see, among others, Yitzhak Arad, *Ghetto in Flames (Jerusalem 1980)*, Dov Levin, *Fighting Back. Lithuanian Jewry's Armed Resistance to the Nazis. 1941-1945* (New York 1985), Chaim Lazar, *Destruction and Resistance* (New York 1985), Reizel Korchak, *Lehavot be'efer* (Merhaviya 1946), Reuben Ainsztein, *Jewish Resistance in Nazi-Occupied Eastern Europe* (London 1974).

[11] Bauer and Rotenstreich, 86.

[12] Levin, 111.

[13] Krzysztof Komarowski, ed., *Armia Krajowa* (Warsaw 1999), 176.

[14] Stanislawa Lewandowska, *Zycie codzienne Wilna w latach II Wojny Swiatowej* (Warsaw 1997), 169.

[15] Ibid, 166.

[16] Ainsztein, 495-6.

[17] Evsey Tseitlin, ed., *The Jewish Museum* (Vilnius 1994), 108.

[18] *Great Soviet Encyclopaedia*, vol. 5 (New York 1974), 518-9.

[19] Ainsztein, 497.

[20] Brayna As, *YIVO bleter. Journal of the Yiddish Scientific Institute*, vol. XXX, no. 2 (Winter 1947), 200.

[21] Sutskever, 192.

[22] Ibid.

[23] Ibid., 184.

[24] Ibid., 192.

[25] Ibid.

[26] Levin, 111.

[27] Yisrael Gutman and Cynthia J. Haft, eds., *Patterns of Jewish Leadership in Nazi Europe. Proceedings of the Third Yad Vashem International Historical Conference.* Jerusalem, April 4-7, 1977 (Jerusalem 1979), 189.

[28] Ainsztein, 510.

[29] Nisl Reznik, Unpublished type script, p. 6.

[30] Korchak, 162.

[31] Sutskever, 193.

[32] Dina Porat, *Me-ever le-gishmi: parashat hayav shel Aba Kovner* (Tel Aviv 2000), 145-46.

[33] See: "Women of Valour: Partisans and Resistance Fighters," by Zhenia Malecki posted on the WEB.

[34] Reznik, 7.

[35] Porat, 147.

[36] Ibid., 148.

[37] Evsey Tseitlin, *Dolgie besedy v ozhidanii schastlivoi smerti* (Vilnius 1996), 50.

[38] Ainsztein, 511.

[39] Ibid., 505.

[40] Gutman, 179.

[41] Rimantas Zizas, "Armed Struggle of the Vilnius Ghetto Jews Against the Nazis in 1942-1944," in E. Zingeris, ed., *The Days of Memory* (Vilnius 1995), 319.

[42] Sutskever, 194.

[43] Lietuvos Ypatingas Archyvas - Lithuanian Security Archives (In the future referred to as L.Y.A.), F. 3377, Ap. 55, B. 52, L. 87. From the interrogation of a certain Mr. Dondes, by a Lithuanian KGB officer, on 14 October 1944.

[44] Arad, 393.

[45] Reznik, 7.

[46] Moshe M. Kohn, ed., *Jewish Resistance During the Holocaust. Proceeding of the Conference on Manifestation of Jewish Resistance.* April 7-11, 1968 (Jerusalem 1972), 164.

[47] Levin, 113.

[48] Porat, 161.

[49] Lucy Dawidowicz, *The War Against the Jews 1933-1945* (New York 1986), 326.

[50] Herman Kruk, *Togbukh fun Vilner geto* (New York 1961), 564.

[51] Bauer and Rotenstreich, 214.

[52] Gutman and Rothkirchen, 424.

[53] Arad, Gutman, and Margaliot, 435-8.

[54] Dworzecki, 387..

[55] Reznik, 8.

[56] Arad, Gutman, and Margaliot, 459-60.

[57] Korchak, 183.

[58] Ibid., 184.

[59] Lazar, 95.

[60] Yehuda Bauer, *A History of the Holocaust* (New York 1982), 268.

[61] Tsvika Dror, ed., *Kvutzat ha-maavak hashniya* (Israel: Ghetto Fighters' House 1987), 140.

[62] Isaac Kowalski, comp. and ed., *Anthology of Armed Jewish Resistance,1939-1945,* vol. 2 (New York 1985), 402.

[63] Porat, 160.

[64] Korchak (1965), 191.

[65] Korchak (1946), 167.

[66] Nisl Reznik, "Geshikhte fun FPO," March 12, 1944, type script, pp. 9-11. Quoted in Lucy S. Dawidowicz, *The War Against the Jews 1933-1945* (New York 1986), 327.

[67] Arad, 433.

[68] Joseph Harmatz, *From the Wings* (Sussex 1998), 80.

[69] Porat, 166.

[70] N.N. Shneidman, *Jerusalem of Lithuania. The Rise and Fall of Jewish Vilnius* (Oakville 1998), 101-4.

[71] Harmatz, 81.

[72] Zizas, 320.

[73] Bauer, 268.

[74] Arad, 417.

[75] Ainsztein, 518.

[76] Ibid., 463.

CHAPTER THREE

[1] Tsvika Dror, ed., *Kvutsat ha-maavak hashniya* (Israel: Ghetto Fighters' House 1987), 40-7.

[2] Ibid. 48

[3] Mark Dworzecki, *Yerushalayim de-Lita in kamf un umkum* (Paris 1948), 462.

[4] Moshe Kalchheim, *Mit shtoltsn gang. 1939-1945* (Tel Aviv 1992), 63-130.

[5] Dworzecki., 393.

[6] Arunas Bubnys, *Vokieciu okupuota Lietuva (1941-1944)* (Vilnius 1998), 264-5.

[7] Longin Tomaszewski, *Wilenszczyzna lat wojny i okupacji. 1939-1945* (Warsaw 1999), 302.

[8] Isaac Kowalski, comp. and ed., *Anthology on Armed Jewish Resistance. 1939-1945*, vol. 2 (New York 1985), 365-8.

[9] Dov Levin, *Fighting Back. Lithuanian Jewry's Armed Resistance to the Nazis. 1941-1945* (New York 1985), 114.

[10] Yitzhak Arad, *Ghetto in Flames* (Jerusalem 1980), 375.

[11] Dror, 70.

[12] Levin, 112. According to another report the group was wiped out by a Polish fascist band. See: L. Eckman and Ch. Lazar, *The Jewish Resistance* (New York 1977), 29.

[13] Dror, 87.

[14] N.N. Shneidman, *Jerusalem of Lithuania. The Rise and Fall of Jewish Vilnius* (Oakville 1998), 83-4 and 97-8.

[15] Baruch Shub, *Me-ever lishmei ha-anana* (Tel-Aviv 1995), 97.

[16] A. Sutskever, *Fun Vilner geto* (Moscow 1946), 199.

[17] Isaac Kowalski, *A Secret Press in Nazi Europe. The Story of a Jewish United Partisan Organization* (New York 1969), 203-4.

[18] Chain Lazar, *Destruction and Resistance* (New York 1985), 84-6.

[19] Lester E. Eckman and Chaim Lazar, *The Jewish Resistance. A History of Jewish partisans in Lithuania and White Russia During the Nazi Occupation 1940-1945* (New York 1977), 35.

[20] Reizel Korchak, *Lehavot be'efer* (Merhaviya 1965), 186.

[21] Arad, 411-3.

[22] Dror, 54.

[23] Ibid., 54-5.

[24] Dina Porat, *Me-ever le-gishmi: parashat hayav shel Aba Kovner* (Tel Aviv 2000), 160.

[25] Moshe M. Kohn, ed., *Jewish Resistance During the Holocaust. Proceedings of the Conference on the Manifestations of Jewish Resistance. Jerusalem, April 7-11, 1968* (Jerusalem 1972), 97.

[26] Levin, 114.

[27] Ibid., 171.

[28] Reuben Ainsztein, *Jewish Resistance in Nazi-Occupied Eastern Europe* (London 1974), 498.

[29] Ibid., 492.

[30] Yisrael Gutman and Cynthia J. Haft, eds. *Patterns of Jewish Leadership in Nazi Europe. Proceedings of the Third Yad Vashem International Historical Conference. Jerusalem, April 4-7, 1977* (Jerusalem 1979), 385.

CHAPTER FOUR

[1] Randolph L. Braham, ed., *Contemporary Views of the Holocaust* (Boston 1983), 10.

[2] Leonard Tushnet, *The Pavement to Hell* (New York 1972), 205.

[3] "Kapitonas Jokubas Gensas. Ados Gensaites prisiminimuose," *Siaures Atenai*, 21 November 1998, no. 42 (436), 3.

[4] Ibid.

[5] Tushnet, 150-3.

[6] "Kapitonas Jokubas Gensas..."

[7] "Keli prisiminimai apie Jokuba Gensa," *Siaures Atenai*, 7 November 1998, no. 40 (434), 3.

[8] Reuben Ainsztein, *Jewish Resistance in Nazi-Occupied Eastern Europe* (London 1974), 505.

[9] Tushnet, 154.

[10] "Keli prisiminimai..."

[11] Tushnet, 140.

[12] Yitzhak Arad, Yisrael Gutman, and Abraham Margaliot, eds., *Documents on the Holocaust* (Jerusalem 1981). 438-40.

[13] Arunas Bubnys, *Vokieciu Okupuota Lietuva. 1941-1944* (Vilnius 1998), 219.

[14] From an interview with Ada Gensaite-Ustijanauskiene on 17 June 2001,

[15] Mark Dworzecki, *Yerushalayim de-Lita in kamf un umkum* (Paris 1948), 467.

[16] Hannah Arendt, *Eichmann in Jerusalem. A Report on the Banality of Evil* (New York 1977), 117.

[17] Dina Porat, "The Justice System and Courts in the Ghettos of Lithuania," *Holocaust and Genocide Studies*, vol. 12, no. 1 (Spring 1998), 61.

[18] L.C.V.A., F. R1421, Ap. 1, B. 39, L. 1,2.

[19] Joseph Harmatz, *From the Wings* (Sussex 1998), 77.

[20] Yisrael Gutman and Cynthia J. Haft, eds., *Patterns of Jewish Leadership in Nazi Europe. Proceedings of the Third Yad Vashem International Historical Conference. Jerusalem, April 4-11, 1977 (Jerusalem 1979), 38.*

[21] Tushnet, 157-8.

[22] Ibid., 161-2.

[23] Ibid., 159.

[24] Dworzecki, 307.

[25] "Sviesesnes akimirkos," *Siaures Atenai*, 23 January 1999, no. 3 (444), 3.

[26] Ibid.

[27] Herman Kruk, *Togbukh fun Vilner geto* (New York 1961), 107-8.

[28] Ainsztein, 699.

[29] Gutman and Haft, 215.

[30] Yehuda Bauer, *A History of the Holocaust* (New York 1982), 161.

[31] Dina Porat.

[32] L.C.V.A., F. R1421, Ap. 1, B. 351, L. 1.

[33] "Sviesesnes akimirkos."

[34] Frances Penney, *I Was There,* translated form the Polish by Zofia Griffen (New York 1988), 77-8.

[35] Ibid. 79.

[36] Ainsztein, 507.

[37] Tushnet, 176.

[38] Arad, Gutman, Margaliot, 440-4.

[39] Ainsztein, 507-8.

[40] Lucy Dawidowicz, *The War Against the Jews 1933-1945* (New York 1986), 285.

[41] Ainsztein, 508.

[42] Arad, Gutman, Margaliot, 449-50.

[43] Moshe M. Kohn, ed., *Jewish Resistance During the Holocaust. Proceedings of the Conference on Manifestations of Jewish Resistance. Jerusalem April 7-11, 1968* (Jerusalem 1972), 218.

[44] Yisrael Gutman and Livia Rothkirchen, eds., *The Catastrophe of European Jewry* (Jerusalem 1976), 441.

[45] Tsvika. Dror, ed., *Kvutsat ha-maavak ha-shniya* (Israel: Ghetto Fighters' House 1987), 93.

[46] Emanuelis Zingeris, ed., *The Days of Memory* (Vilnius 1995), 302.

[47] Arad, Gutman, Margaliot, 453-4.

[48] Avraham Tory, *Surviving the Holocaust. The Kovno Ghetto Diary* (Cambridge, Mass. 1990), 490.

[49] Dawidowicz, 326.

[50] Eric Sterling, "The Death of Resistance Hero Yitzhak Witenberg and the

decline of the United Partisan Organization," in Ruby Rohrlich, ed., *Resisting the Holocaust* (Oxford 1998), 60-5.

[51] Yitzhak Arad, *Ghetto in Flames* (Jerusalem 1980), 383.

[52] Moshe Shutan, *Geto un vald* (Tel-Aviv 1971), 150.

[53] According to A. Tory the Jew with the gun was stopped on his way out from the ghetto. See Avraham Tory, 409.

[54] Ainsztein, 505-6.

[55] Tushnet, 198-9.

[56] Ibid., 196.

[57] Chaim Lazar, *Resistance and Destruction* (New York 1985), 104.

[58] Arunas Bubnys, 219.

[59] From an interview with Ada Gensaite-Ustijanauskiene on 17 June 2001.

[60] Chaim Lazar, 104.

Bibliography

1. Agranovskii, G., and I. Guzenberg. *Litovskii Ierusalim*. Vilnius 1992.
2. Ainsztein, Reuben. *Jewish Resistance in Nazi-Occupied Eastern Europe*. London 1974.
3. Arad, Yitzhak. *The Partisan: From the Valley of Death to Mount Zion*. New York 1979.
4. _____. *Ghetto in Flames: The Struggle and Destruction of the Jews in Vilna in the Holocaust*. Jerusalem 1982.
5. Arad, Yitzhak, Yisrael Gutman, and Abraham Margaliot, eds. *Documents on the Holocaust*. Jerusalem 1981.
6. Arendt, Hannah. *Eichmann in Jerusalem. A Report on the Banality of Evil*. New York, 1977.
7. Atamukas, S. *Lietuvos Zydu Kielas*. Vilnius 1998.
8. Bauer, Yehuda. *They Chose Life: Jewish Resistance in the Holocaust*. New York 1973.
9. _____. *A History of the Holocaust*. New York 1982.
10. Bauer, Yehuda, and Nathan Rotenstreich, eds. *The Holocaust as Historical Experience*. New York 1981.
11. Beinfeld, Solon. "Health care in the Vilna Ghetto," *Holocaust and Genocide Studies*. Vol. 12, no. 1 (Spring 1998), 66-98.
12. Braham, Randolph L., ed. *Contemporary Views of the Holocaust*. Boston 1983.
13. Cohen, Israel. *Vilna*. Philadelphia 1992.
14. Dawidowicz, Lucy. *The War Against the Jews. 1933-1945*. New York 1975.
15. _____. *A Holocaust Reader*. New York 1976.
16. Dror, Tsvika, ed. *Kvutsat ha-maavak ha-shniya*. Ghetto Fighters' House, Israel 1987.
17. Dworzecki, Mark. *Yerushalayim de-Lita in kamf un umkum*. Paris 1948.
18. Eckman, Lester E., and Chaim Lazar. *The Jewish Resistance: A History of the Jewish Partisans in Lithuania and White Russia During the Nazi Occupation. 1940-*

1945. New York 1977.

19. Erlich, Rachel. *Imposed Jewish Governing Bodies Under Nazi Rule*. YIVO *Colloqium. December 2-5, 1967*. New York 1972.

20. Fleming, Gerald. *Hitler and the Final Solution*. Berkeley 1984.

21. Gefen, M. ed. *Sefer ha-partizanim ha-yehudim*. Vol. 1. Tel-Aviv 1958. Vol. 2, Merhaviya, Israel 1959.

22. Gensaite-Ustijanauskiene, Ada. Interviews. *Siaures Atenai*. Vilnius. 7 November 1998, no. 40, 3; 21 November 1998, no. 42, 3, and 23 January 1999, no. 3, pp.3,9.

23. *Great Soviet Encyclopaedia*, vol. 5. New York 1974.

24. Greenbaum, Masha. *The Jews of Lithuania. A History of a Remarkable Community. 1316-1945*. Jerusalem 1995.

25. Grobman, Alex, and Daniel Landes, eds. *Genocide: Critical Issues of the Holocaust*. Chappaqua, New York 1983.

26. Grodzienski, A. I. *Vilna Almanac* (Wilno 1939). Republished and edited by Issac Kowalski. New York 1992.

27. Gutman, Yisrael, and Cynthia J. Haft, eds. *Patterns of Jewish Leadership in Nazi Europe. Proceedings of the Third Yad Vashem International Historical Conference. Jerusalem, April 4-7, 1977*. Jerusalem 1979.

28. Gutman, Yisrael, and Livia Rothkirchen, eds. *The Catastrophe of European Jewry*. Jerusalem 1976.

29. Harmatz, Joseph. *From the Wings*. Sussex 1998.

30. Hilberg, Raul. *The Destruction of the European Jews*. New York 1985.

31. Kalchheim, Moshe, ed. *Mit shtoltsn gang*. Tel Aviv 1992.

32. Kalmanovitch, Zelik. *Yoman be-geto Vilna*. Tel-Aviv 1977.

33. Klee, E., W. Dressen, V. Ries. *The Good Old days*. New York 1988.

34. Kohn, Moshe M., ed. *Jewish Resistance During the Holocaust. Proceedings Of the Conference on Manifestations of Jewish Resistance . Jerusalem, April 7-11, 1968*. Jerusalem 1972.

35. Korchak, Reizl. *Lehavot be-efer*. Merchaviya, Israel 1946.

36. Kowalski, Isaac. *A Secret Press in Nazi Europe. The Story of the Jewish United Partisan Organization*. New York 1969 .

37. _____, ed. *Anthology of Armed Jewish Resistance. 1939-1945*. Vol. 2. New York 1985.

38. Kruk, Herman. *Togbukh fun Vilner geto*. New York 1961.

39. Lazar, Chaim. *Destruction and Resistance*. New York 1985.

40. Levin, Dov. *Fighting Back: Lithuanian Jewry's Armed Resistance to Nazis 1941-1945.* New York 1985.

41. Lewandowska, Stanislawa. *Zycie codzienne Wilna w latch II Wojny Swiatowej.* Warsaw 1997.

42. *Masines zudynes Lietuvoje (1941-1944). Dokumentu rinkinys.* Vilnius 1965.

43. Penney, Frances. *I Was There.* Translated from the Polish by Zofja Griffen. New York 1988.

44. Porat, Dina. *Me-ever le-gishmi: Parashat hayav shel Aba Kovner.* Tel Aviv 2000.

45. _____. "The Justice System and Courts of Law in the Ghettos of Lithuania," *Holocaust and Genocide Studies.* Vol. 12, no. 1 (Spring 1998), 44-65.

46. Posierbska, Helena. *Wilenskie Ponary.* Gdansk 1999.

47. Rindzyunski, Aleksander. *Hurban Vilna.* Tel Aviv 1987.

48. Reznik, Nisl. Unpublished type script entitled "Geshikhte fun F.P.O." (Personal evidence on the history of the F.P.O.), written in March 1944 and passed on to the Yiddish writer Shmerke Katsherginski on 12 October 1944. Copy of the document in my possession.

49. Rohrlich, Ruby, ed. *Resisting the Holocaust.* Oxford 1998.

50. Rozauskas, E., ed. *Documents Accuse.* Vilnius 1970.

51. Rudashevski, Yitskhok. *The Diary of the Vilna Ghetto. June 1941-April 1943.* Tel Aviv 1973.

52. Sachar, Howard Morley. *The Course of Modern Jewish History.* New York 1963.

53. Schur, Grigorij. *Die Juden von Wilna.* Munchen 1999.

54. Shneidman, N.N. *Jerusalem of Lithuania. The Rise and Fall of JewishVilnius.* Oakville 1998.

55. Shub, Baruch. *Me-ever lishmei ha-anana.* Tel-Aviv 1995.

56. Shutan, Moshe. *Geto un vald.* Tel-Aviv 1971.

57. Suhl, Yuri, ed. *They Fought Back.* New York 1975.

58. Sutskever, A. *Fun Vilner geto.* Moscow 1946.

59. Tomaszewski, Longin. *Wilenszczyzna lat wojny i okupacji1939-1945.* Warsaw 1999.

60. Trunk, Isaiah. *Judenrat: The Jewish Councils in Eastern Europe Under Nazi Occupation.* New York 1977.

61. Tseitlin, Evsey. *Dolgie besedy v ozhidanii schastlivoi smerti.* Vilnius 1996.

62. _____, ed. *The Jewish Museum.* Vilnius 1994.

63. _____ . *The Jewish Museum. Vilnius Ghetto: Lists of Prisoners.* 2 vols.

Vilnius 1996-8.

64.Tushnet, Leonard. *The Pavement to Hell.* New York 1972.

65. Yahil, Leny. *The Holocaust: The Fate of European Jewry 1932-1945.* New York 1990.

66. *YIVO bleter.* Vol. XXX, no. 2. Winter 1947.

67. Zingeris, Emanuelis, ed. *The Days of Memory.* Vilnius 1995.

Appendicies

ORIGINAL ARCHIVAL DOCUMENTS:
I. 18 July 1941. Letter about the creation of a ghetto in Vilnius.
II. 29 April 1942. Vilnius ghetto Jewish police Regulations, issued by the office of the Gebietskommissar.
III. 18 June 1942. Letter about the number of prisoners in the Jewish ghetto jail, and the reasons for their arrest.
IV. 15 August 1942. Letter of the Head of the Vilnius ghetto, J. Gens, to the Head of the Vilnius District Lithuanian Administration.
V. 5 November 1942. Order of the Gebietskommissar about the use of Jewish workers.
VI. 17 January 1943. List of books taken out by the Head of the Vilnius ghetto, J. Gens, from the Jewish ghetto library.
VII. List of Vilnius ghetto Jewish policemen who were allegedly involved in criminal activity against fellow Jews. List produced after the liberation of Vilnius from Nazi occupation, sometimes in the mid 1940s.

I.

Letter (in Lithuanian) from K. Kalendra, Manager for Internal Affairs, Vilnius City Administration, to the Vilnius City Committee, about the creation of a ghetto for the Jews of the city. It is stated in the letter that an appropriate district for the ghetto has already been selected, and that this district is currently inhabited by 10,224 people, 78 per cent of them Jewish. The ghetto is intended for 20,000 Jews, all other Jews from the region are to be removed. The letter is dated 18 July 1941.

Source: LCVA, F. R643, Ap. 3, B. 4152, L. 71

```
VILNIAUS MIESTO IR SRITIES
VIDAUS REIKALŲ VALDYTOJAS                                    71.
      ------
   1941 m.liepos mėn. 18...d.
     Nr 48              Vilniaus Miesto   K o m i t e t u i
       V i l n i u s

                   Liečia: žydų klausimą

                          1) Jau nustatytojo žydų kvartalo (ghetto)
                   techniška paruošimą, aptvėrimą ir tikslių ribų
                   nustatymą vykdo Miesto Savivaldybės skirtas
                   techniškasis personalas inž.-urbanisto vado-
                   vybėje. Tuo tarpu vykdomi paruošiamieji dar-
                   bai, tikslus ghetto planas ir medžiaga aptvė-
                   rimui.
                          Nustatytame kvartale šiuo metu gyvena
                   10.224 žmonės, kurių 78% žydų.
                          2) Esamų krautuvių ir bazių bei sandė-
                   lių dislokacijai ryšium su ghetto steigimu,
                   vykdo Prekybos Skyrius. Prekybos Skyrius vyk-
                   dys ir toliau ghetto prekėmis aprūpinimo pla-
                   ną. Numatoma, kad ghetto turės nustatytą kie-
                   kį krautuvių ir sandėlių. Prekės bus pristato-
                   mos į ghetto sandėlius urmu ir ilgesniam lai-
                   kui, pagal žydams nustatytas normas.
                          3) Kiti ghetto įrengimai kaip ligoninės,
                   prieglaudos, kepyklos nekelia jokio susirūpi-
                   nimo, nes minėtame kvartale yra tam tikslui
                   pakankamai patalpų.
                          4) Ryšium su p.Komendanto pasiūlymu
                   įsteigti ghetto 20000 žydų, gi likusius iš-
                   gabenti iš Vilniaus srities. Miesto savival-
                   dybė jau turi suorganizavusi žmonių kadrus,
                   kurie vykdys žydų persikėlimo bei likusio
                   turto surašymo darbus.
                          Priede: ghetto planas.

                                 /pas/ K. Kalendra.
                              VIDAUS REIKALŲ VALDYTOJAS
```

II.

Vilnius Ghetto Jewish Police Regulations.
Source: LCVA, F. 643, Ap. 3, B. 3000, L. 109
Quoted from E. Rozauskas, ed., Documents Accuse (Vilnius 1970), 172-4.

No. 69

The Gebietskommissar of
the City of Vilnius
No. II/2 A 91 M/K.

Vilnius, April 29, 1942.

To
Herr Buragas
Municipality of Vilnius
V i l n i u s

In the enclosure I forward to you the directives for the employment of Jewish police. I ask you to control the implementation of these directives. In case of offence against the directives you are requested to inform me.

p. p. *Murer*

Encl.: 1 page.

LTSR CVA, f. 643, ap. 3, b. 300, l. 109. Original.

No. 70

Directives for the Employment of the Jewish Police

In accordance with the principle that the Jewish population has to settle its affairs itself all orders of the Gebietskommissar of the City of Vilnius are to be implemented with the help of the Jewish police. The Lithuanian guards are only a supervisory body. The directives for the Jewish police are as follows:

1. The Jewish police is under the direction of the Chief of the Jewish police, Jacob Gens.
2. Under the direction of its police chief the Jewish police has to look for order and security in the ghetto.

3. Its paramount task is to carry into effect all the orders and directives of the Gebietskommissar for the City of Vilnius, without any reservations. Accountable to me are the chief of the Jewish police installed by me and the respective policemen in charge of a task.

4. The following directions must be implemented with special accuracy:

   a) Only Jews who are employed at a certain work and who want to go to their work place can leave the ghetto.

   b) In the absence of a special permit of the Gebietskommissar the columns of workmen can leave the ghetto between 6 and 9 a. m. only. The return from the place of employment must take place between 3 and 8 p. m.

   c) Visits by Jews from the Kailis workers' block to the ghetto and vice versa are prohibited. No exit is permitted on Sundays or public holidays, unless to some assigned job.

   d) Strange Jews who are not registered at the ghetto as well as other people who want to go into hiding there are not to be admitted to the ghetto. They are to be apprehended and turned over to the Security Police.

   e) Orders by offices and persons which will be carried out in the workshops of the ghetto need my permission. Bills for work performed in the ghetto are to be submitted to me before delivery.

   f) The employment of Jewish labour is permitted with a few exceptions only in groups of ten and more. Therefore Jews can appear in the streets of Vilnius only in columns of ten and more. The ghetto police patrols are to control and secure the observance of the present regulation. Individual Jews who are to be employed alone have also to join a column while on their way to their place of employment.

   g) Working Jews are to be placed under a column leader who is responsible for the behaviour of the

Jews on the way to their place of employment and
for adequate productivity there. The column leader
has to see to it that the Jews under him do not buy
food or accept it as a gift and that no such food be
brought to the ghetto.

h) The guard at the ghetto gate has to see to it that
neither food nor other consumer goods whatsoever
be brought into the ghetto without the permission of
the Gebietskommissar.

i) The right to supply food have specially authorized
firms only. In case Lithuanian or German offices including the Wehrmacht force Jews to take food or
other goods to the ghetto the food and goods are to
be secured by the Jewish ghetto police. The amount
of food and goods thus taken into the ghetto as well
as the names of offices which had ordered this are
to be reported to me.

j) The ghetto gate is to be under constant supervision
by two policemen. Moreover during the return of the
Jews into the ghetto the gate is to be guarded by an
adequate number of police officers permitting proper
control.

k) The guard journal has to show precisely what Jewish officials were on duty at a given hour at the
ghetto gate.

5. Jews, column leaders and Jewish policemen will be
punished with death in case they commit any offence
against the regulations issued by the Gebietskommissar
of the City of Vilnius.

The Gebietskommissar of the City of
Vilnius

p. p. *Murer*

Vilnius, April 29, 1942.

III.

Letter (in Lithuanian) from to Head of the Vilnius Jewish ghetto jail to the Lithuanian officer in charge of Jewish affairs in the Vilnius city administration, about the number of prisoners in the ghetto jail, and the reasons for their arrest, on 18 June 1942, 8:00 a.m.

Source: LCVA, F. R643, Ap. 3, B. 30, L. 2.

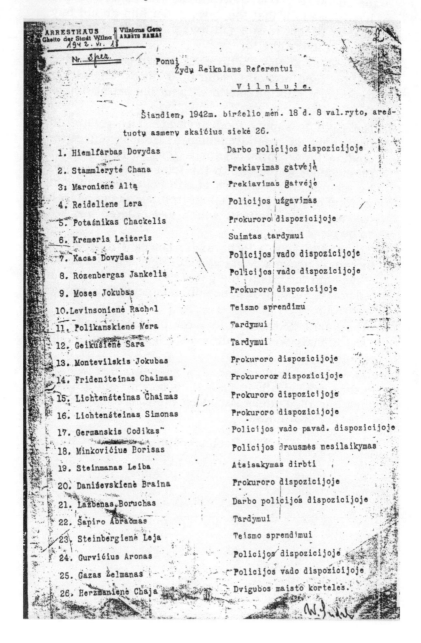

IV.

Letter (in Lithuanian), dated 15 August 1942, from the Head of the Vilnius Ghetto, Jacob Gens, to the Head of the Lithuanian Vilnius District Administration, requesting permission to set up a camp, in the district of Vilnius, for the Jewish workers who were to be involved in cutting wood for the heating needs of the ghetto.

Source: LCVA, F.R685, Ap.4, B.40, L.272.

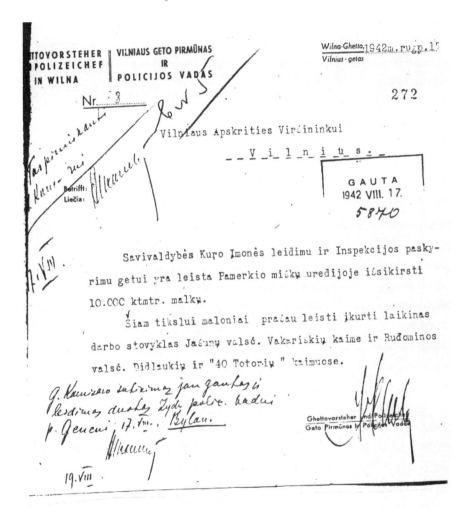

V.

Order (in German) of the Vilnius City Gebietskommissar about the use of Jewish work-force.

Source: LCVA, F. R 1421, Ap. 1, B. 4, L. 1-2.

English Translation:

Vilnius, 5 November 1942.

I.   General. The Vilnius ghetto is under the exclusive jurisdiction of the Gebietskommissar. Any association or communication with Jews, not related to their work is forbidden.

II.   Requests for Jewish workers are to be directed to the Labour Office at the Gebietskommissar. Jewish workers brigades are to consist of at least ten workers, and be supervised by a foreman appointed by the ghetto Jewish authorities. In extreme cases permission may be granted for single Jewish workers to be employed. Single Jews walking to, or from, work without special permits, issued by the Labour Office will be arrested. Jews are forbidden to leave their place of work at lunch time.

Without the permission of the Labour Office no Jew may be transferred from one place of work to another. Without special permission of the Labour Office no Jew can be employed out of town. It is forbidden to employ Jews as physicians, dentists, nurses, druggists, as well as hairdressers, barbers, messengers, delivery men, or house help. The employers are to make sure that Jews are not involved in procuring food, or other daily life necessities, while at work.

Jews are to be employed full time. They are to leave the ghetto between six and nine a.m. and return to the ghetto between three and eight p.m. In cases when a Jew is employed at a night shift, special permission from the Labour Office is required.

III.   Jewish workers are to be paid according to the following rates:

   a) men over sixteen   RM 0,15 per hour
   b) women over sixteen   RM 0,125 per hour
   c) youths under sixteen   RM 0,10 per hour

IV.   Jewish workers are provided with work permits by the Labour Office of the Gebietskommissar. Employers are forbidden to issue work permits.

V.   The employers are required to inform the Labour Office when a Jewish worker is no longer employed.

VI.   The Labour Office retains the right to transfer Jewish specialists from place to place.

VII.   Institutions and work places which disobey this order will be charged, and deprived of the possibility to employ Jewish workers in the future.

BESTIMMUNGEN

über den Einsatz der jüdischen Arbeitskräfte.

I. Allgemeines.

1. Das Wilnaer Ghetto steht unter der Aufsicht des Gebietskommissars der Stadt Wilna. Dieser ist allein weisungsberechtigt, und für alle Fragen, die das Ghetto betreffen, zuständig.

2. Der ausserdienstliche Verkehr mit Juden, sowie jede Privatunterhaltung und die Betreibung von Geschäften, ist strengstens verboten. Die hierfür erlassenen Strafbestimmungen gelten sowohl für die Reichsdeutsche als auch für die einheimische Bevölkerung.

II. Arbeitseinsatzbestimmungen.

3. Die Vermittlung von jüdischen Arbeitskräften erfolgt durch die Dienststelle „Der Gebietskommissar in Wilna -ARBEITSAMT-" (Wilnaerstr. 10, Zimmer 6, Fernruf 661, 3422, 3423). Anträge auf Zuweisung von jüdischen Arbeitskräften sind daher nur an das Arbeitsamt zu richten.

   Eigenmächtiges Anwerben von jüdischen Arbeitskräften ist untersagt.

4. Eine Verpflichtung des Arbeitsamts, jüdische Arbeitskräfte zur Verfügung zu stellen, besteht nicht.

5. Der Einsatz der jüdischen Arbeitskräfte erfolgt grundsätzlich nur in Kolonnen von mindestens 10. Der Einsatz von einzelnen jüdischen Arbeitskräften kann ausnahmsweise nur dann erfolgen, wenn diese durch einheimische Arbeitskräfte nicht zu ersetzen sind. Die Entscheidung darüber liegt beim Arbeitsamt.

6. Die in einer Kolonne von 10 und mehr eingesetzten Juden haben unter Führung eines von der Arbeitsabteilung im Ghetto bestimmten jüdischen Kolonnenführers geschlossen die Arbeitsstätte aufzusuchen und zurückzukehren.

7. Juden in Stärke von weniger als 10 haben grundsätzlich nur in Begleitung eines Beauftragten der Dienststelle oder Betriebes die Arbeitsstätte aufzusuchen und zurückzukehren.

   Falls eine Begleitung durch die Dienststelle oder den Betrieb nicht möglich ist, kann das Arbeitsamt einen besonderen Passierschein für das Betreten der Strassen ohne Begleitung ausstellen.

8. Die Passierscheine werden nur vom Arbeitsamt Wilna ausgestellt.

   Den Dienststellen und Betrieben ist es verboten Passierscheine auszustellen.

9. Einzelne Juden, die auf den Strassen ohne Passierscheine angetroffen werden, machen sich strafbar und werden verhaftet. Die Dienststellen und Betriebe dürfen daher Juden ohne Begleitung oder ohne Passierschein des Arbeitsamts nicht zum Betreten der Strassen veranlassen.

10. Juden dürfen ihre Arbeitsstätte während der Beschäftigungszeit und während der Mittagspause nicht verlassen.

11. Das Ausleihen oder die Abgabe von jüdischen Arbeitskräften ist ohne Genehmigung des Arbeitsamts verboten.

12. Den Dienststellen und Betrieben ist untersagt ohne Genehmigung des Arbeitsamts jüdische Arbeitskräfte ausserhalb von Wilna zu beschäftigen.

13. Die Verwendung der einzelnen jüdischen Arbeitskräfte zu irgendwelchen bevorzugten Hilfsdiensten bei der Wehrmacht und zivilen Dienststellen hat zu unterbleiben.

   Juden dürfen ihrem Beruf als Krankenbehandler (Aerzte, Zahnärzte, Apotheker, Hebammen, Krankenschwester u. s. w.) und Friseure für Arier nicht ausüben. Ebenso ist der Einsatz der Juden im Haushalt und als Botengänger für Besorgungen verboten.

   Für Wehrmachtsdienststellen ist die Verfügung des Wehrmachtbefehlshabers Ostland vom 20. 9. 1941 massgebend. Diese hat unter anderem folgenden Wortlaut:

164ª

R121 n. 1 b. 4 l. 2

Jegliche Zusammenarbeit der Wehrmacht mit der jüdischen Bevölkerung, die offen oder versteckt in ihrer Einstellung deutschfeindlich ist, und die Verwendung von einzelnen Juden zu irgendwelchen bevorzugten Hilfsdiensten für die Wehrmacht hat zu unterbleiben. Ausweise, die den Juden ihre Verwendung für Zwecke der Wehrmacht bestätigen, sind durch militärische Dienststellen keinesfalls auszustellen".

14. Die Dienststellen und Betriebe haben dafür Sorge zu tragen, daß die bei ihnen beschäftigten Juden keine Geschäfte betreiben und zu verhindern, daß sie Lebensmittel, Holz u. a. m. einkaufen und in das Ghetto mitnehmen. Die Mitnahme von Bedarfsgütern, insbesondere von bewirtschafteten Artikeln, ist strengstens untersagt.

15. Beschwerden, die den Arbeitseinsatz der jüdischen Arbeitskräfte betreffen, sind zwecks Bestrafung an das Arbeitsamt zu richten.

16. Die Arbeitszeit der jüdischen Arbeitskräfte ist ganztägig. Sie müssen das Ghetto in der Zeit von 6—9 Uhr verlassen und ab 15 Uhr bis spätestens 20 Uhr zurückkehren.

   In Fällen, wo eine normale Arbeitszeit nicht möglich ist. (z. B. Nachtschicht) bedarf es der vorherigen Genehmigung des Arbeitsamts.

III. Entlohnung.

17. Die beschäftigten jüdischen Arbeitskräfte haben Anspruch auf Lohn und zwar:

   a) Männer vom 16. Lebensjahr aufwärts — RM 0,15 pro Std.
   b) Frauen — RM 0,12½
   c) Jugendliche unter 16 Jahre — RM 0,10

   Zivile Dienststellen, private Betriebe, Genossenschaften usw, mit Ausnahme der deutschen Dienststellen und der Stadtverwaltung Wilna, haben denselben Betrag, der an die Juden gezahlt wird, an die Kasse des Gebietskommissars Wilna Stadt (Gediminostr. 3, Zimmer 9) einzuzahlen oder zu überweisen (Bankkonto bei der Reichskreditkasse oder bei der Sparkasse in Wilna).

18. Akordlöhne sind für die jüdischen Arbeitskräfte im Allgemeinen nicht erwünscht; in Ausnahmefällen erteilt hierzu die Genehmigung das Arbeitsamt.

IV. Arbeitsausweise.

19. Die jüdischen Arbeitskräfte sind mit Ausweisen des Gebietskommissars in Wilna -Arbeitsamt- (früher Sozialamt) versehen.

20. Die Dienststellen und Betriebe sind nicht berechtigt, diese Ausweise den Juden abzunehmen.

21. Bei Einstellung und Entlassung einer jüdischen Arbeitskraft ist die Dienststelle oder der Betrieb verpflichtet, in den Ausweis die entsprechenden Vermerke zu machen.

V. Entlassungen.

22. Die Dienststellen und Betriebe sind verpflichtet, die Entlassung von jüdischen Arbeitskräften vorher dem Arbeitsamt zu melden, damit ein zweckentsprechender Arbeitseinsatz gewährleistet ist.

23. Auf Verlangen des Arbeitsamts sind namentlich zu benennende jüdische Arbeitskräfte aus der Dienststelle oder dem Betrieb sofort zu entlassen.

VI. Umsetzung.

24. Dem Arbeitsamt steht das Recht zu, berufsfremd eingesetzte jüdische Facharbeiter umzusetzen, ohne dafür Ersatz zur Verfügung zu stellen.

VII. Schlussbestimmungen.

25. Die Dienststellen oder Betriebe, die gegen diese Bestimmungen verstossen, werden zur Verantwortung gezogen und von einer weiteren Zuteilung jüdischer Arbeitskräfte ausgeschlossen.

26. Meine Richtlinien und Merkblatt für den Einsatz der jüdischen Arbeitskräfte vom 7. April 1942 werden ausser Kraft gesetzt.

DER GEBIETSKOMMISSAR DER STADT WILNA.

Wilna, den 5. November 1942.

Staatsdruckerei Auschra" Wilna. 578M/612

VI.

List of books (in Yiddish) taken out by the Head of the Vilnius ghetto, Jacob Gens, from the Jewish ghetto library. The list includes, among others, prose fiction books by the Jewish writers Anski, Apatoshu, Bergelson, Sholom-Aleikhem, and Zinger, as well as the Jewish History by H. Graetz, and four volumes of the Jewish Encyclopaedia in Russian. Dated 17 January 1943. Source: LCVA, F. R-1421, Ap. 1, B. 351, L. 1.

VII.

List (in Russian) of Vilnius ghetto Jewish policemen who participated in criminal activities against the Jewish population.

This list includes forty nine names. Six were shot by the Germans. Seven were shot by the Soviet partisans. Three were tried and convicted by Soviet courts. Five left for Poland. One was arrested by the Soviet authorities. One perished in a concentration camp in Estonia.

"This list includes the names of/Jewish/policemen who in some way participated in activities aimed against the Jewish population. It is possible to assume, with some justification, that many of the policemen whose fate still remains unclear perished. After the liquidation of the Vilnius ghetto almost all of them were confined to various concentration camps almost/all of them/ were destroyed.

This list is compiled on the basis of information and documented materials provided by com. S. Garbelis who was sent into the Jewish ghetto police by the underground/communist/ party Committee."

This list is signed by Gutkovich, Director of the Jewish Museum in Vilnius, and dated sometime in the mid forties.

Source: LCVA, F. R1421, Ap. 1, B. 39, L. 1-2

СПИСОК

ПОЛИЦЕЙСКИХ ВИЛЬНЮССКОГО ГЕТТО, ПРИНИМАВШИХ УЧАСТИЕ В ПРЕСТУПНЫХ 34,
ДЕЙСТВИЯХ ПРОТИВ ЕВРЕЙСКОГО НАСЕЛЕНИЯ.

№ п/п	Фамилия , имя	Что известно о его судьбе
1.	Авербух Айзик	Растрелян немцами
2.	Бак Липман	
3.	Бернштейн Исак	Растрелян партизанами
4.	Блох Самуил	
5.	Блох Шимон	
6.	Цельник Сруль- Нисон	Уехал в Польшу
7.	Хилевич Бер	
8.	Димитровский Абрам	Уехал в Польшу
9.	Деслер Давид	Расстрелен немцами
10.	Древин Ное	
11.	Срухт Изидор	
12.	Фишер Давид	
13.	Фридман Исаяш	
14.	Гронер Гуго	Расстрелян немцами
15.	Геня Яков	Расстрелян немцами
16.	Ицкович Абрам	Расстрелян партизанами
17.	Ицкович Теа	
18.	Косельзон Вигдор	
19.	Лейбман Янкель	Погиб в концлагере в Эстонии
20.	Левас Меер	
21.	Лурье Эльяш	
22.	Марголис Урьяш	
23.	Мушкат Иосиф	
24.	Нусбаум Марьян	
25.	Остер Рафаил	
26.	Слейский Лазарь	Уехал в Польшу
27.	Пузериский Мовес	Рестован Советскими властями
28.	Рок Леон	

Еврейский Музей
в Вильнюсе
_____ 194 г.
№ _____

№ п/п	Фамилия, имя		Что известно о его судьбе
29.	Ревеньская Эльзбета	....	
30.	Ринг Нахман	....	Расстрелян партизанами
31.	Радошицкий Еуда	....	
32.	Зайдель Вульф	....	
33.	Шапиро Самуил	....	
34.	Штейн Пейсах	....	
35.	Смольговский Мовес	....	Расстрелян немцами
36.	Товбин Ицхок	....	
37.	Выткоский Мовес	....	
38.	Зальштейн Вульф	....	Растрелян партизанами
39.	Желязо Израиль	....	
40.	Вальцвасер Людвик	....	Расстрелян партизанами
41.	Невес Александр	....	Расстрелян партизанами
42.	Шварц Берг	....	Расстрелян партизанами
43.	Мешчанский	....	Осужден Советским судом
44.	Кердман	....	Осужден Советским судом
45.	Марголис Менахим	....	Уехал в Польшу
46.	Савер Зельман	....	Уехал в Польшу
47.	Шапиро Генрих	....	Осужден Советским судом
48.	Розенталь	....	
49.	Обергарт Вальтер	....	Расстрелян немцами

В настоящий список включены те полицейские, которые в какой-либо форме принимали участие в преступных действиях против еврейского населения. В отношении тех полицейских, о судьбе которых ничего не известно можно вполне законно полагать, что многие из них погибли, ибо после ликвидации Вильнюсского гетто, почти все они находились в различных кон лагерях, где почти были уничтожены. Список составлен на основании д документальных материалов и информации, полученной от тов. С. Гарбели, направленного в еврейскую полицию гетто подпольным Комитетом партии.

Директор
Еврейского Музея ...   ЛУТКОНИХ

Index

Tory, A., 125
Tushnet, Leonard, 129
Ulpis, Antanas, 32
Usas, Colonel, 107
Vaitkevicius, Juozas, 58
Vigodsky, Dr. Jacob, 18
Vitas, Juozas (Juozas Valunas), 55, 58, 59
Voroshilov, Marshal K., 57
Wehrmacht, 5, 11, 18, 20, 23-25, 35, 36, 83, 107, 133
Weiss, Martin, 119, 130, 131
Wiesenthal, Shimon, 97
Willa, *Unterscharfuhrer,* 47
Witenberg, Yitzhak, x, xi, 34, 35, 43-78, 88, 90, 126-128, 135-139
Wladyslaw IV, King, 7
Yiddishists, viii, 8, 9, 26
YIVO (Jewish Scientific Research Institute), 8, 31, 32, 131
Ypatingas Burys (Sonderkommando), 13
Yung Vilne (Young Wilno), 9
Zhabotinsky, V., 106
Zinger, 117
Zionists, ix, 8-10, 26, 48, 50, 64, 82-85, 136; Zionist-Revisionists, ix, 48, 50, 85, 106, 125, 136
Ziskovitch, 70, 71
Zlotnik-Sheinbaum, Pesia, 83, 84, 95, 96

AGMV Marquis

MEMBER OF SCABRINI MEDIA

Quebec, Canada
2002